ROBERT FROST

••

ROBERT FROST

Elaine Barry

A Frederick Ungar Book

CONTINUUM • NEW YORK

1988

The Continuum Publishing Company
370 Lexington Avenue
New York, NY 10017

Third Printing

Copyright © 1973 by Frederick Ungar Publishing Co., Inc.

Printed in the United States of America

Designed by Anita Duncan

Library of Congress Catalog Card No. 72-79942
ISBN 0-8044-2016-5

Grateful acknowledgment is made to Holt, Rinehart and Winston, Inc. for
the reprinting of material from

THE POETRY OF ROBERT FROST *edited by Edward Connery Lathem.* Copyright 1916,
1923, 1928, 1930, 1934, 1939, 1943, 1945, 1947, 1949, © 1967, 1969 by Holt,
Rinehart and Winston, Inc. Copyright 1936, 1942, 1944, 1945, 1947, 1948,
1950, 1951, 1952, 1953, 1954, © 1955, 1956, 1958, 1959, 1960, 1961, 1962 by
Robert Frost. Copyright © 1964, 1967, 1970 by Lesley Frost Ballantine.

SELECTED LETTERS OF ROBERT FROST *edited by Lawrance Thompson.* Copyright
© 1964 by Holt, Rinehart and Winston, Inc.

LETTERS OF ROBERT FROST TO LOUIS UNTERMEYER. Copyright © 1963 by Holt,
Rinehart and Winston, Inc.

SELECTED PROSE OF ROBERT FROST *edited by Hyde Cox and Edward Connery Lathem.*
Copyright 1939, 1954, © 1960, 1967 by Holt, Rinehart and Winston, Inc.
Copyright 1946, © 1959 by Robert Frost. Copyright © 1956 by The Estate of
Robert Frost.

THE DIMENSIONS OF ROBERT FROST *by Reginald L. Cook.* Copyright © 1958 by
Reginald L. Cook.

The reprinting of portions of unpublished letters is made with the permission
of The Estate of Robert Frost, Alfred C. Edwards, Executor.

For John, Tom, Jim, and Anne

Acknowledgments

I am indebted to the American Council of Learned Societies for financial assistance that enabled me to do the research for this book; in particular, I should like to thank Dr. Richard Downar, Director of the American Studies Program, for his courtesy and helpfulness at all times. To those forbearing colleagues and friends with whom I discussed and tried out interpretations of Frost's poems, to Barbara Calton and Gail Ward, who typed the final manuscript with cheerful efficiency, and to Lina Mainiero, my understanding and capable editor, I am deeply grateful. My dearest debt is to my brother, Father John E. Barry O.S.A., whose incisive comments on the manuscript had a delight and wisdom all their own.

Contents

	Chronology	ix
1	*Introduction . . . Mostly Biographical*	1
2	*The Lyric Voice*	19
3	*The Dramatic Narrative*	47
4	*Frost and the Sonnet Form*	79
5	*The Meditative Voice . . . Some Major Themes*	99
	Notes	131
	Bibliography	135
	Index	139

Chronology

1874:   Robert Frost is born in San Francisco on 26 March.

1885:   His father dies, Robert and his sister Jean are taken by their mother to live in New England.

1892:   Frost graduates from Lawrence High School, sharing the valedictorian honors with class-mate Elinor White. In September, he enters Dartmouth College, but stays less than a semester.

1895:   Frost marries Elinor White in December.

1896:   In September their first child, Elliott, is born.

1897:   Frost enrolls at Harvard as a special student but leaves after eighteen months.

1898:   A daughter, Lesley, is born.

1900:   The Frosts move to a farm in Derry, New Hampshire, bought by his paternal grand-father. Their son, Elliott, dies.

1902:   A son, Carol, is born.

1903:   A fourth child, Irma, is born.

1905:   A fifth child, Marjorie, is born.

1906–1911:   Financial pressures force Frost to take a teaching position at the Pinkerton Academy in Derry.

1907:   A sixth child, another daughter, is born, but dies within two days.

1912:   In September, the Frost family leaves for England.

1913:   Frost's first book, *A Boy's Will*, is published by David Nutt and Company, London.

1914:   His second volume, *North of Boston*, is published in London by the same publisher.

1915:   The outbreak of World War I forces Frost to bring his family back to the United States.

1916:   *Mountain Interval* is published in New York by Henry Holt & Co., who remain Frost's publishers throughout his life.

1921:   Frost takes up a one-year appointment at the University of Michigan as Poet in Residence. For most of his remaining years, he is to hold academic posts at various American universities.

1923:   *New Hampshire* is published and is awarded the Pulitzer Prize the following year.

1928:   Frost publishes *West-Running Brook*.

1930:   The first edition of *Collected Poems* appears, and is awarded the Pulitzer Prize of 1931.

1934:   Frost's much-loved daughter Marjorie, who had married in Montana the previous year, dies after childbirth.

1936:   *A Further Range* is published, winning a third Pulitzer Prize for Frost.

1938:   Elinor Frost dies.

1939:   An enlarged edition of *Collected Poems* appears.

1940:   Frost's son, Carol, commits suicide.

1942:   The publication of *A Witness Tree* wins Frost a fourth Pulitzer Prize.

1945:   *A Masque of Reason* is published.

1947:   *A Masque of Mercy* and *Steeple Bush* are published.

1949:   A third edition of *Complete Poems* appears, again enlarged. (A definitive edition, *The Poetry of Robert Frost*, edited by Edward Connery Lathem, was published in 1969.)

1958:   He is appointed consultant in poetry at the Library of Congress.

1961:   Frost participates in the inauguration ceremony of President Kennedy.

1962:   He publishes *In the Clearing* and makes a good-will trip to Russia under the auspices of the State Department.

1963:   Frost dies in Boston on 29 January at the age of eighty-eight.

1

◆◆◆◆◆◆◆◆◆◆◆◆◆◆◆◆◆◆◆◆◆◆◆◆◆◆◆◆◆◆◆◆◆◆◆

Introduction
. . . Mostly Biographical

A voice said, Look me in the stars
And tell me truly, men of earth,
If all the soul-and-body scars
Were not too much to pay for birth.
                    —*"A Question"*

The years since the death of Robert Frost in 1963 have seen a radical change in the public estimation of him. When Lionel Trilling, at a dinner to celebrate Frost's eighty-fifth birthday in 1959, spoke of the "terror" of Frost's poetry, he raised a storm of controversy. Today, what surprises us about the incident is the public reaction. Few would now dispute that Frost was indeed "one acquainted with the night" and that many of his speculations place him in the great tradition of New England writers—Hawthorne, Melville, James—who penetrated the dark undersurface of American life.

Poems such as "Stopping by Woods" or "The Road Not Taken," with which Frost's image was stereotyped for so long, are being replaced in anthologies by lesser-known and infinitely stronger poems such as "The Subverted Flower" or "Directive" or "The Most of It." His letters—released for publication only after his death—are now recognized as having literary merit in their own right, as being as honest, whimsical, and poetic as those of Emily Dickinson. Finally, the myth that Frost created around his own personality—the conservative, optimistic, homespun philosopher who traveled miles to keep promises—has been badly shaken by the first two volumes of the official biography, Lawrance Thompson's *Robert Frost: The Early Years*, and *Robert Frost: The Years of Triumph*. Perhaps in the first swing of the pendulum from idealization to disillusionment there is a danger of overemphasizing Frost's personal failures. What really matters for the reader is that he fulfilled his ambition to "lodge a few poems where they will be hard to get rid of, to lodge a few irreducible bits." More than a few.

Robert Frost was born in San Francisco in 1874. His father belonged to an old New England family and worked as a journalist and political manipulator on the West Coast; he died when Robert was eleven. Robert's mother, Isabelle Frost, a Scottish immigrant with a strong, if unorthodox, religious temperament, had a much more profound influence on him. He pays tender, compassionate tribute to her in the poem "The Lovely Shall Be Choosers," in which her lonely life is seen in terms of seven ironic "joys," which the fates dispense to her. After their father's death Robert and his sister Jean were brought to New England by their mother. So, at the impressionable age of eleven, Robert Frost had to learn a way of life and a way of speech that were strange to him. The experience perhaps sharpened his observation and his sense of critical detachment. Years later, after he had lived in England and had his first two books published there, he noted in a letter:

I wonder if coming to New England from as far away as California can have had anything to do with my feeling for New England and I wonder if my having written so much about it from as far away as old England can have helped.[1]

In New England, the family received a dutiful, but hardly warm, welcome from the older Frosts, the children's grandparents. Isabelle Frost hastily set out to create an independent existence for herself and her children by teaching in various schools; eventually she ran a small private school in Lawrence, Massachusetts. Robert attended Lawrence High School. By 1892 the future looked bright for him. He was graduating from high school with distinction, sharing the valedictorian honors with a classmate, Elinor White. He had already published a couple of poems in the school magazine. His grandfather had agreed to help him financially through Dartmouth College. And he was in love with Elinor White.

But the bright promise proved ephemeral. In place of confidence and optimism came instability and self-questioning. Frost left Dartmouth without even completing a semester, and drifted from job to job—mill hand, journalist, teacher in his mother's school. His restlessness was temperamental, but it was accentuated by two factors, each of which brought to the surface traits of his character that have relevance to his poetry.

One was the fact that Elinor insisted on postponing their plans of marriage and had left to attend Saint Lawrence University in Canton, New York. Frost felt betrayed and insecure and dramatized his emotions with youthful extravagance. In one flamboyant gesture, he had five of his poems privately printed and bound in an edition of two, called it, symbolically, *Twilight,* and made a special trip to see Elinor at Saint Lawrence and present her copy to her. She took the slim volume that was thrust into her hands but did not stay to talk to him. As he returned in dejection, he tore up and threw away his copy of the book—thus making the one surviving copy of *Twilight* the most valuable item in the collector's industry that has grown up around his work. In a more curious but equally flamboyant gesture of emotional indulgence, he headed off, without advising anyone of his whereabouts, to the Dismal Swamp in Virginia, entered its terrifying wilderness, and wandered there without map or compass until he met by chance a party of hunters. What was the point of such a Byronic gesture? The enactment of a death wish? A childish desire to make Elinor feel guilty for her stubbornness? Or simply the adolescent self-dramatization that is described in "Into My Own"? At any rate, themes of betrayal, of fear, of loss of love, of being "bereft," are strong in Frost's poetry.

The second factor that contributed, as cause or effect, to Frost's restlessness in these years, was his distrust of formal education. He claimed that he left Dartmouth "to be educated"; he later left Harvard after spending less than two years there. This distrust of academic knowledge was to be carried through his entire life. The man who was awarded more than forty honorary degrees never bothered to earn a degree himself. He liked to set up a contrast between the smart-aleck knowledge of the college boy and the wise common sense of the self-reliant countryman. And one of his favorite poses was that of the philosopher-farmer, rich in the wisdom of nature, disdainful of "Greenwich Village talk." His attitude to formal education may be right, of course; and Frost was certainly very well-read. But it could have been an excuse for mental laziness, and it left him open to the charges of Yvor Winters and, later, George Nitchie, that Frost was a "spiritual drifter," that he failed to attain the stature of W. B. Yeats, T. S. Eliot, or Wallace Stevens because he lacked the intellectual discipline to construct a coherent system of thought and fell back instead on isolated perceptions and defensive whimsy.

In 1895 Frost married Elinor White and in 1900, after a few years of teaching and studying, he began farming in Derry, New Hampshire, on a farm that had been bought for him by his grandfather. In the first twelve years of marriage the Frosts had six children, but only four—a son and three daughters—survived. The death of their oldest son from cholera at the age of four was particularly heartbreaking. The ravages that his death created in the relationship of Robert and Elinor Frost are partly suggested in "Home Burial."

Despite Frost's image as a farmer-poet, the Derry sojourn was the only time in his life when he relied solely on farming for his income. Financial pressure forced him back to teaching in 1906. Yet during the lonely years in Derry he read deeply in poetry and wrote many of the poems that were later to be collected in *A Boy's Will*. Nor was his talent as unrecognized as Ezra Pound was later to imply. As early as 1894 the influential New York newspaper *The Independent* published the first poem Frost sent to it ("My Butterfly"), and the editor assumed the role of a kind of patron to Frost, giving him both advice and publishing space. Frost was sufficiently sure of what he was trying to do to reject the advice; he was still searching for his distinctive poetic voice. It would be less a matter of what he said than how he said it. He was sure that poetry should not be "musical" in the current fashion, yet "sound" was of the essence. "Yes, I think sound is an element of poetry, one but for which imagination would become reason," he wrote to the literary editor of *The Independent* back in 1894.[2]

Impulsive as ever, Frost took the gamble, in 1912, of devoting all his time to poetry. His grandfather had left him the Derry farm in his will, and Frost sold it in 1911, as soon as he was legally able to do so. With the money from this, plus a small annuity from his grandfather's estate, plus a gambling spirit, Frost sailed with his family to England. For the first time in his life he had the opportunity of discussing poetry and poetic theories with other poets, and he relished it. Though he was too much the individualist to ally himself with any group, he met many of the Georgians (Lascelles Abercrombie, Wilfred Gibson, F. S. Flint, Edward Thomas) and the imagists (T. E. Hulme, Ezra Pound), and a new intellectual excitement is found in his letters written at this time. Here at last his theories about poetry became clear, and he found the distinctive voice for which he had been searching. The difference between *A Boy's Will* (which had been written mostly in Derry) and his next book, *North of Boston* (mostly written in England), reflects as abrupt a change as can be found in any poet's work. With few exceptions the poems in *A Boy's Will* could have been written by any of the Georgians. But no one could mistake the distinctive Frostian voice of "Mending Wall," "A Servant to Servants," "Home Burial," or "The Wood-Pile" in *North of Boston*. It was as if Frost needed to rub his ideas up against conflicting ones before he could define his beliefs at all. England was a catalyst for him: it gave him the chance to discuss his poetry with people who were interested. It gave him, too, the confidence and excitement of being able to find his own poetic mode, and a publisher for his first two books. World War I forced him back home in 1915. At the age of thirty-nine, with a wife and four children to provide for, he was fixed on a career in poetry.

By the time Frost landed in America he was

beginning to receive critical attention, and he set out cannily to establish his reputation among reviewers and anthologists. There is something of the finesse of a modern public-relations expert in the way he went about cultivating the good will of Amy Lowell, who had a formidable literary eminence in Boston, or William Braithwaite, a critic on the influential *Boston Evening Transcript*. Throughout his life Frost was to accept adulation uncritically, make use of people who could help his reputation, and refuse to listen to criticism. He never outgrew a vanity about his poetry or a petulance toward his detractors.

Farming and poetry still could not provide him with an adequate income. In 1916 he was given help by the greatest of all modern patrons—the American university system. For the rest of his life Frost held the position of poet-in-residence or visiting professor at many of the leading colleges—notably Amherst, Dartmouth, Harvard, and the University of Michigan. He became almost as well-known for his public readings and lectures as he was for his poems. Meanwhile he continued to produce volumes of poetry, four of which won Pulitzer Prizes. What is remarkable about his poetic output is not its size but its range and its consistency of quality. So many poets, after a brief burst of creative activity, fade into silence, mediocrity, or repetition. Frost could write a poem as fine as "Directive" in his seventies.

Frost's private world, however, darkened as his public image grew brighter. His sister, Jean, in and out of mental institutions most of her life, died in 1929. His son Carol committed suicide in 1940. Two of his daughters made ill-fated marriages that ended in divorce. His youngest daughter—whom

Frost called "the noblest of us all"—died of septice-
mia after giving birth to her first child. Most telling
of all Frost's personal tragedies was the death of his
wife in 1938. Their relationship had always been
complex—intense, loyal, but plagued by their temperamental differences, by the demands of Robert's
possessiveness and egotism, and by the bitterness of
Elinor's resentful silences. Lawrance Thompson records that, when Elinor was dying, Frost paced up
and down outside her door, hoping she would send
for him, give him some indication that their forty-
three years together had been worth "all the soul-
and-body scars." She never did.

Little of this personal tragedy is reflected in
Frost's poetry, except in a general way—in themes of
loss, of the arbitrariness of fate, of the difficulties of
finding one's human significance. Frost was not a
"confessional" poet. Indeed, he had a positive dis-
taste for making poetic capital out of private
griefs. Writing to Louis Untermeyer about Untermeyer's marital agonizings after he had divorced
his second wife to remarry his first one, Frost warned
him:

I'd impose it as a penalty on you that you shouldn't wax
literary on what you have been through—turn it to account
in any way. . . . It must be kept away down under the surface where the great griefs belong. I don't mean you must
stop writing, but you must confine yourself to everything
else in the world but your own personal experience. . . .
The thought would be too much for me of all three of you
putting up a holler in verse about it all. The decencies
forbid you should score off it.[3]

Frost lived on for twenty-five years after Elinor's
death, and they were years of increasing public

recognition. Under the auspices of the U. S. State Department he was sent on good-will missions to England and Russia. Congress voted him a Congressional Medal. Honorary doctorates—including ones from Oxford and Cambridge—were showered on him. He allied himself to no poetic trend, was disdainful of most of his fellow poets—yet the American public regarded him as its spokesman. When he read at the inauguration of John F. Kennedy, he appeared almost as a folk hero, the embodiment of frontier American individualism, as solid as New England granite, affirming the old-fashioned values of national faith and pride: "The land was ours before we were the land's." On his death in January 1963, he was indeed the national poet that Walt Whitman had dreamed of being.

Perhaps the best way to an understanding of Frost's poetic intentions and achievements is through a line that occurs near the end of one of his dramatic narratives, "The Mountain" (1914).* The poem is largely a dialogue between a visitor to the mountain of the title and a man who has lived his whole life at its base. As the beautifully subtle dialogue progresses, the mountain man reveals his fascination with a spring on top of the mountain, which he has heard about but has never seen, that has the extraordinary reputation of being hot in winter and cold in summer. Both the towering, inscrutable mountain and the Grail-like spring are rich in metaphysical

---

* The date assigned to any poem throughout this book is the date of its first publication, whether in a periodical or a volume. It is not necessarily, of course, the date of writing.

association, and the poem has much to say about the
nature of faith and scientific knowledge. But at the
end of the poem, when he is quizzed again about the
mysterious spring, the mountain man admits lacon-
ically and a little shamefacedly:

> "I don't suppose the water's changed at all.
> You and I know enough to know it's warm
> Compared with cold, and cold compared with warm.
> But all the fun's in how you say a thing."

For Frost, the way "you say a thing" circum-
scribes all reality. In a few words, the spring has
suddenly dropped its mystery and allure, and the
old mountain man, with nothing more to say now
that the fancy has been dispelled, moves on. The act
of creating poetry, of "saying things," is the act of
creating meaning. A good poem should end, Frost
claimed, in a "clarification of life." He never ceased
to be concerned with the relationship between intuited
truth and the verbal shapes that contain it, between
perception and conceptualization.

Yet if words are our reality they are also our
delight. The emphasis, after all, is on "the fun." In
so many of his poems Frost is concerned with "performance." ("The whole thing is performance and
prowess and feats of association.") Almost all of his
poems are experiments in "tones of voice," ways of
"saying a thing," and even the most seemingly direct
of them should be approached through the persona of
the implied speaker—whether it is the simple way-
farer of "Stopping by Woods," barely verbalizing
the nature of his temptation, or the more rational
and practical tongue-in-cheek farmer of "Mending
Wall," who sees the absurdity of what he is doing

but does it anyway, or the subtly intellectual speaker of "For Once, Then, Something." The characterization of a speaking voice was Frost's buffer between himself and a subject that might otherwise become sentimental, trite or melodramatic.

As he wrote in a letter to Lewis Chase in 1917:

I was afraid I hadn't imagination enough to be really literary. And I hadn't. I have just barely enough to imitate spoken sentences. I can't keep up any interest in sentences that don't *shape on some speaking tone* of voice. I'm what you would call reproductive. I like best (in my poetry at least) not to set down even an idea that is of my own thinking: I like to give it as in character when I am drawing character.[4]

Without a proper attention to the speaking voice of Frost's poems, we may well get his subjects out of perspective. How many of us, for example, first read "The Road Not Taken" as a serious, if wistful, comment on the irrevocable decisions that govern our lives? Frost himself was fond of teasing his readers on their gullibility here ("I bet not one reader in ten knows what 'The Road Not Taken' is about"). He once declared that the most perceptive question anyone ever raised with regard to the poem was "Why the 'sigh'?" in the line "I shall be telling this with a sigh." The "sigh," of course, helps to characterize the "I," and provides the first hint that the poem is a gentle parody of the kind of person whose life in the present is distorted by nostalgic regrets for the possibilities of the past, who is less concerned for the road taken than for the "road not taken." (The speaker was modeled on the English poet Edward Thomas, who, after any country walk with Frost, would lament all the wildflowers that might have been seen on some other road.) Once we have the initial clue, all other parts of the characterization seem obvious: the negative emphasis in the title, the nostalgic, autumnal mood, the hesitancy of the decision ("Though as for that, the passing there/Had worn them really about the same"), the inability to turn his back completely on any possibility ("Oh, I kept the first for another day!"), the romantic pose of finality in the last line ("And that has made all the difference"). Our awareness of the characterization of a speaker has altered the meaning of the poem.

Similarly it is only a close attention to the voice-tones of the characters in "The Witch of Coös" that enables us to see that poem, not simply in tragic psychological terms (as it is usually seen), but as belonging to the same tradition of folk comedy— albeit black comedy—to which Faulkner's *As I Lay Dying* belongs.

If the meaning of a Frost poem is often inextricably related to the voice of its persona and his way of "saying a thing," nowhere is this more evident than in those poems where the voice is, in the broadest sense, a "humorous" one. Very few of Frost's poems deal with characters or situations that are objectively comic. But in a great many, a potentially serious theme is deliberately channeled into a resolution that is ironic, whimsical, or playful: one thinks, for instance, of poems as thematically different as "Birches," "Come In," or even "Directive." The speakers of such poems tend to be self-deprecatory, literally afraid of taking themselves seriously, given to a "throwaway" mode of expression that has become something of a Frostian trademark.

The attitude of mind behind such whimsicality, however, is often fundamentally serious. Frost was aware of the abstract value of humor as a way of looking at, and coping with, the world. He saw it quite literally as a saving grace, anchoring one to sanity and human wholeness.

In the preface Frost wrote in 1935 to the post-humous edition of Edwin Arlington Robinson's *King Jasper*, he analyzed perceptively the role that humor can play in the process of artistic creation. Frost obviously felt a temperamental sympathy with the way Robinson handled the "griefs" of his poetry. Robinson's ironic humor, he claimed, was a gallant and stoic defense as he reached down to "immedicable woes"; not for him to bleed his heart out self-pityingly all over poetry's pages:

He knew how to forbid encroachment. And there is solid satisfaction in a sadness that is not just a fishing for minis-tration and consolation. Give us immedicable woes—woes that nothing can be done for—woes flat and final. And then to play. The play's the thing. Play's the thing.[5]

The "play" behind the voice of so many of Frost's personas is dictated by the same moral im-perative. It represents for Frost a kind of stoicism, an aversion to "putting up a holler in verse" about his own "immedicable woes." Working from Robin-son's poignant ironies, Frost laid down an equation of good taste that he applied strictly to his own poetry:

The style is the man. Rather say the style is the way the man takes himself; and to be at all charming or even bear-able, the way is almost rigidly prescribed. If it is with outer seriousness, it must be with inner humor. If it is with outer humor, it must be with inner seriousness. Neither one alone without the other under it will do.[6]

But, although no one has paid more tender tribute to the genuine moral strength of Robinson's ironic personas, Frost was open-eyed enough to recognize the human and poetic limitations of the humorous style, even his own.

Many sensitive natures have plainly shown by their style that they took themselves lightly in self-defense. They are the ironists. . . .

I own any form of humor shows fear and inferiority. Irony is simply a kind of guardedness. So is a twinkle. It keeps the reader from criticism. . . . Humor is the most engaging cowardice. With it myself I have been able to hold some of my enemy in play far out of gunshot.[7]

The best thing of all, he recognized, is "belief," belief that lies beyond the need of defenses, humorous or otherwise. This is what the great poets have. "Belief is better than anything else, and it is best when rapt, above paying its respects to anybody's doubt whatsoever. At bottom the world isn't a joke."[8] What is important is not simply to have "belief" (Frost in fact had plenty), but, poetically, to make no apology for having it. Not, at any rate, the kind of apology that lies behind the ironic personas of so many of Frost's serious poems.

"Humor is the most engaging cowardice." Although Frost's manner is not always humorous, and although much of his ironic defensiveness represents, as we shall see later, a conscious pragmatism, an awareness of the moral and psychological value of a humorous perspective, this statement perhaps sums up best of all why Frost is not among the great poets, though he is among the very good ones. We reserve greatness for "believers"—in no matter what. Frost's concern "not to set down an idea that is of [his] own thinking," but rather "to give it as in character" certainly made for liveliness, immediacy, and variety in his work. He greatly extended the "sound" of poetry. But all too often the "voice" of a poem acts as a mask, "simply a kind of guarded-ness," shielding the poet from the full implications of his serious subjects and preventing any real intellectual grappling with them.

It would be a mistake, of course, to assume that in every Frost poem the voice is humorous or whimsical, or indeed that a persona is clearly characterized at all. In some poems there are no idiosyncrasies of voice to render personality, no intruding touches of characterization. In such poems as "Design," for instance, or "Neither Out Far Nor In Deep," Frost is more concerned with the subject than with the speaker's apprehension of it, and there is a direct commerce between poet and reader. Whether or not Frost is using his "own" voice here is debatable. Suffice it to say that in some of Frost's poems we are unaware of an individualized persona taking delight in "saying a thing," but that most of his poems do "shape on some speaking tone of voice," and that an awareness of "voice" is perhaps the most fruitful way of approaching his poetry.

Apart from the interpretation of individual poems, a proper attention to the tones of voice in his poetry enables us to appreciate more exactly the nature of Frost's distinctive contribution to American literature. The sheer variety of sound in Frost's poetry makes most other poets seem one-dimensional.

Working with the cadences of New England speech, and declining "music" in favor of "the sound of the talking voice," Frost ranged in tone from the lyric to the narrative, from the dramatic to the meditative, from the "terrifying" to the humorous. All the fun's in how you say a thing.

2

The Lyric Voice

The aim was song.
—*"The Aim Was Song"*

In the preface that Frost wrote to Edwin Arlington Robinson's *King Jasper*, he praised Robinson's discovery of "old ways to be new." The phrase is revealing. It would seem to affirm Frost's basic conservatism, his impatience with all the new-fangled poetic modes and theories that marked the 1920s and 1930s. Yet the emphasis is as much on "new" as it is on "old." A poem, Frost claimed, had to be "new," presenting a fresh insight, an original response:

[A poem] begins in delight and ends in wisdom. The figure is the same as for love. No one can really hold that the ecstasy should be static and stand still in one place. It begins in delight, it inclines to the impulse, it assumes direction with the first line laid down, it runs a course of lucky events, and ends in a clarification of life—not necessarily a great clarification, such as sects and cults are founded on, but in a momentary stay against confusion.[1]

To achieve this "clarification" with any degree of honesty, moreover, the expression had also to be original, personal, "new." As Frost wrote to Louis Untermeyer in 1918, criticizing Edgar Lee Masters's popular *Spoon River Anthology*: "All I know with any conviction is that an idea has to be a little new to be at all true and if you say a thing three times it ceases to be so."[2]

What, then, does Frost mean by his praise of "old ways to be new"? He is simply differentiating between a genuine poetic "newness," which is "a clarification of life," and a meretricious newness, where the clarification is lost in the distractions of technical virtuosity. "Delight" must be thought out— freshly and without clichés—before it can become "wisdom." And the process of thinking it out involves the stern old-fashioned discipline of poetic form. For Frost, theme and technique, "truth" and expression, are inextricably one.

In many of Frost's own best-known poems, he falls back on the oldest of old ways to be new—the lyric. The lyric is as old as Greek poetry. It is, by definition, a short personal poem. But its most essential characteristic is its musicality, achieving its musical effects by traditional techniques of meter, rhyme, and stanzaic patterning. Much of Frost's reputation rests on his lyrics—on poems such as "Stopping by Woods," "Acquainted with the Night," "Reluctance," and "The Road Not Taken." And perhaps his choice of a mode that had been sanctioned by centuries of use may blind us to the fact that he not only extended the subject matter of lyric poetry but also brought extraordinary sophistication and originality to that important ingredient of music.

Frost's attitude to music in poetry was more ambiguous than he cared to admit. Time and again he protested that music and poetry were quite separate art forms, that the intrusion of musical concepts in discussing poetry only clouded a poem's distinctively poetic achievement, that what was really important was the nonmetrical sound of "the talking voice." And yet, for all such protestations, Frost was a skillful and highly conscious prosodist, concerned not only for "sound" in a poem, but, more specifically, for what he called "tune." "Tune" is the aesthetic appeal to the ear that a good poem has, an effect that comes very largely from the musical regularity of meter. Nothing demonstrates this concern better than Frost's lyric poetry. The title of one of his lyrics sums it up: "The Aim Was Song."

The sound of such an early lyric as "Reluctance," the concluding poem in *A Boy's Will* (1913), for instance, is predominantly musical in the traditional sense:

> Out through the fields and the woods
> > And over the walls I have wended;
> I have climbed the hills of view
> > And looked at the world, and descended;
> I have come by the highway home,
> > And lo, it is ended.
>
> The leaves are all dead on the ground,
> > Save those that the oak is keeping
> To ravel them one by one
> > And let them go scraping and creeping
> Out over the crusted snow,
> > When others are sleeping.
>
> And the dead leaves lie huddled and still,
> > No longer blown hither and thither;
> The last lone aster is gone;
> > The flowers of the witch hazel wither;
> The heart is still aching to seek,
> > But the feet question "Whither?"
>
> Ah, when to the heart of man
> > Was it ever less than a treason
> To go with the drift of things,
> > To yield with a grace to reason,
> And bow and accept the end
> > Of a love or a season?

The speaker in this poem is a youthful romantic, creating his pose of world weariness in the traditional manner of youthful romantics. Yet it *is* a pose, and the pose demands that he "sing" rather than "talk." Hence the language is deliberately poetic

("I have wended," "Ah, when"). There is even a
faint biblical echo ("And lo, it is ended") to under-
score the self-dramatizing mood of consummation.
The rhyme is regular, like a song, with little hint of
an everyday speaking voice. There is a softness, a
hint of wistful falling-away, in the feminine endings
of the rhymes ("treason," "reason," "season"). The
whole poem conveys a tone similar to that in Yeats's
"The Stolen Child"—the sense of delicate melancholy
that dominates so much *fin-de-siècle* poetry. And, although the speaker of "Reluctance" remains questioning rather than despairing, too positive to be
content with simple escape, there is, for Frost, no
conflict at any time between the demands of capturing the tones of the persona's voice and the demands
of creating melodious sound.

The poem is a beautifully sustained mood piece,
and much of its effect rests in the manipulation of its
cadences to suggest the subdued sadness of finality.
The images are quite traditional, as we might expect
from this speaker—the end of a journey and the
end of a season. But note the subtle way in which
the sound of the poem supports the effect of the
imagery: the way the theme of finality is emphasized
by the shortening of the final line in each stanza,
where the usual three-foot line brakes to two beats to
give the effect of a slowing-down ("And lo, it is
ended"). Or the way the attenuation of the rhyme-
scheme in each stanza seems to create its own sense
of "reluctance," as the rhyme is held over for an
extra two lines.

The mood is resolved in the final stanza; a resolution that is subtly underlined by a return to
metrical regularity after the slowness of the previous stanza:

Ah, when to the heart of man
    Was it ever less than a treason
To go with the drift of things,
    To yield with a grace to reason,
And bow and accept the end
    Of a love or a season?

By now the human relevance of the autumnal metaphor is made explicit. The real emotional pivot of the poem is not the end of a season at all but the end of a love. Yet the word "love" is only introduced in the last line, slipped in casually, with a certain diffidence. It is this diffidence on the part of the speaker that saves the poem from the sentimentality that its conventional images and musical cadences have brought it close to. He is self-indulgent, certainly, seeing in nature a reflection of his own mood, but he has enough tact not to belabor the comparison. And he has enough detachment to reach a resolution of his mood.

The resolution may not be very affirmative—it is, after all, "reluctant"—but inasmuch as it is a general formulation of a problem, an enlarging of it beyond a self-centered relevance to the speaker alone to a broader comment on "the heart of man," it is a resolution. Though it may seem a "treason" to the "aching" heart, the inevitable will be accepted by the speaker with all those gestures of formal courtesy ("yield with a grace," "bow and accept") that man has created to hold annihilation at bay.

"Reluctance" is the work of a consummate lyricist: in it theme, metaphor, meter, rhyme, and structure are inseparable. But the sound is not distinctively Frostian. It is an exercise in traditional form, giving no indication at all of the "tones of the speaking voice" that he claimed, in letters written at the time, he was seeking to capture. The sounds of the talking voice are more obvious in the dramatic narratives of his next book, *North of Boston.* Yet even in the lyrics he continued to write, especially in those written after *A Boy's Will,* Frost consciously moved away from the traditional "singing" form to a more complex view of what constituted "tune" in poetry. The secret, he claimed, was to capture the rhythms of everyday talk (the intonations that give real meaning to a sentence—what he called "the sound of sense") and then blend these rhythms with the regular beat of meter:

An ear and an appetite for these sounds of sense is the first qualification of a writer, be it of prose or verse. But if one is to be a poet he must learn to get cadences by skillfully breaking the sounds of sense, with all their irregularity of accent across the regular beat of the metre.[3]

Rhythm without meter leads to the trite simplicities of free verse, which Frost despised all his life ("like playing tennis with the net down"); meter without rhythm leads to childish singsong. Through theorizing and experimenting, Frost developed a sophisticated understanding of these basic elements of poetry.

In the blending of rhythm and meter in a poem, Frost always emphasizes the sense of strain: "I am never more pleased than when I can get these into strained relation. I like to drag and break the intonation across the meter as waves first comb and then break stumbling on the shingle."[4] The tension that arises in a poem from this "straining" of technical elements both parallels and embodies the conceptual tension in which any poem comes to creation. A poem, he once explained to Louis Untermeyer, begins as "a tantalizing vagueness," simply "a lump in the throat, a sense of wrong, a homesickness, a lovesickness." It then has to find its "thought," and "the thought finds the words." But the process is not magical. It involves all that intellectual strain by which any vague feeling is distilled into communicable form. Honesty and discipline are crucial to the process. Frost was not exaggerating its difficulty when he claimed, years later, that "it takes a hero to make a poem."

This interrelatedness of thematic and technical tension is evident in a much later lyric, "Come In" (1941). There is an ambivalence in the persona of this poem that makes him a more mature, less self-indulgent, character than the speaker of "Reluctance"; and his ambivalence sets up that tension between the demands of natural speech rhythm and the demands of meter that Frost considered so important for lively poetry. The musical cadences of "Reluctance" would have been totally inappropriate for this speaker.

The poem deals with a favorite Frost theme—the "death wish" attraction of the dark, the pull of lonely places, the call to "come in/To the dark and lament." Just why this is such a major preoccupation in Frost's poetry is another question altogether. Most thinking people have felt the attraction of oblivion; most romantic poets have given expression to it. For Frost the attraction was sharp and poignant. As a poet he himself could resist such attraction by the act of creating a poem, and perhaps this is partly what he meant when he described poetry as "a momentary stay against confusion." Through the personas in his poems Frost dramatizes various resolutions to this pull of the dark. The speaker of "Into My Own," for instance, indulges the temptation with grandiose self-dramatization. In "Stopping by Woods" he rejects it, with a certain self-righteousness ("The woods are lovely, dark and deep / But I have promises to keep"). In "Come In" he is more assured, more likeable, more jocular. He is able to verbalize his attraction for the bird singing in the depths of the dark wood and set it at a distance in a tentative metaphor ("almost like a call").

> As I came to the edge of the woods,
> Thrush music—hark!
> Now if it was dusk outside,
> Inside it was dark.
>
> Too dark in the woods for a bird
> By sleight of wing
> To better its perch for the night,
> Though it still could sing.
>
> The last of the light of the sun
> That had died in the west
> Still lived for one song more
> In a thrush's breast.
>
> Far in the pillared dark
> Thrush music went—
> Almost like a call to come in
> To the dark and lament.
>
> But no, I was out for stars:
> I would not come in.
> I meant not even if asked,
> And I hadn't been.

The thrush in this poem is the inverse of Keats's nightingale. Where Keats's bird represents an eternal principle of joy, in contrast to the blighted, sorrowful, transitory life of man, here the thrush sings a song of "lament" in the "dark" and invites man to join it. Indeed, for the speaker the temptation to do so is real enough: the "darkness" is mentioned in every stanza, and the call, as the title emphasizes, is to "come in," far more enticing and personal than "go in." The song is a siren song. But the speaker is sufficiently in control of the temptation to notice the limitations of this darkness. It is constricting: the bird cannot fly in it to "better its perch for the night" by any "sleight of wing." And the word "pillared" suggests not only the secure refuge of a church but, especially to a man who was "out for stars," the confinement of a prison. He makes his choice without any qualms:

> But no, I was out for stars:
> I would not come in.
> I meant not even if asked,
> And I hadn't been.

This call and its rejection, then, provide the emotional tension of the poem. What makes it a successful poem is largely that the emotional tension is echoed in, and reinforced by, a metrical tension. Throughout the poem Frost demonstrates his ideal of keeping the natural rhythm of speech and the regular rhythm of meter in "strained relation." The very sound of the speaker's voice thus sets up its own resistance to the invitation. The meter is basically anapestic, but from the first stanza it is continually being broken as the speaker's assertiveness comes through:

> As I came to the edge of the woods,
> Thrush music—hark!
> Now if it was dusk outside,
> Inside it was dark.

We are pulled up, as he is, by the force of "thrush music." Yet the immediate directive—"hark!" —puts him in control of the situation, while also, because of its archaic flavor, suggesting a certain jocularity, a mock solemnity to counteract the real solemnity. So does the "outside/inside" juxtaposition immediately following, where the natural speech rhythm takes over. Idiom and rhythm have combined to individualize the speaker and remove any suggestion of a singsong effect.

This healthy jocularity is carried throughout the poem. It is there, for instance, in the neat word play of the bird bettering its perch by "sleight of wing." And it is there in the typically throwaway style of the last two lines, where the real significance of the bird's invitation—the fascination with the dark—is parried by treating it as simply a social invitation. It is this unobtrusive characterization through rhythm and tone that puts such a distinctively Frostian stamp on this lyric. The resolution, both emotional and technical, is stronger and more individual than in "Reluctance."

"Reluctance" and "Come In," then, demonstrate Frost's concern for "tune" in his poetry, and the increasing subtlety of his interpretation of the word as it relates more and more to the sound of a talking, rather than a singing, voice. It is a concern that is evident in all his work. At the same time, the two poems also demonstrate the dramatic ways in which rhythm and meter can characterize the personas of his lyrics. What such an emphasis on voice and characterization achieved was an extraordinary diversity of tone and subject within the traditional lyric poem.

"Bereft" (1927) suggests something of this diver-

sity. It portrays a bleak realization of absolute loneliness, a sudden, despairing sense of loss. Lawrance
Thompson gives the biographical background to the
poem.[5] In 1893, while Frost was courting Elinor
White, he spent the summer with her family at an old
colonial farmhouse in Salem, New Hampshire. It was
a tense and uncertain time in the relationship. Frost
had given up his chance of a college education at
Dartmouth, convinced that he could educate himself
better informally. Jealous that Elinor might fall in
love with somebody else while she was away at
Saint Lawrence University, he spent most of the
summer trying to persuade her to leave college and
marry him. At the end of the summer, when the
Whites left the farmhouse, Frost announced that he
would stay on alone for a few days, partly no doubt to
indulge his own self-pity, partly perhaps to make
Elinor sorry for his lonely plight. At night, alone in
the big house he was gripped by the fear that he captures more than thirty years later in "Bereft."

> Where had I heard this wind before
> Change like this to a deeper roar?
> What would it take my standing there for,
> Holding open a restive door,
> Looking downhill to a frothy shore?
> Summer was past and day was past.
> Somber clouds in the west were massed.
> Out in the porch's sagging floor
> Leaves got up in a coil and hissed,
> Blindly struck at my knee and missed.
> Something sinister in the tone
> Told me my secret must be known:
> Word I was in the house alone
> Somehow must have gotten abroad,
> Word I was in my life alone,
> Word I had no one left but God.

The effect of psychological terror is largely gained, as in any good thriller, by projecting an animistic, threatening quality on to the physical surroundings. The shore is "frothy"; the clouds are "somber"; the wind is roaring. Both the day and the summer, with all their sense of fruitful fulfillment, are "past," leaving the speaker exposed to the incertitudes of a wintry night. There is "something sinister" in the sound of the leaves. The sense of malevolence in the landscape is extended even to the house itself, which provides no haven. The door is "restive," the porch "sagging."

All of this might seem a melodramatic overstatement were it not for the fact that the speaker has worked himself up to a paranoiac sense of terror. He sees the leaves like a snake rising to strike him, and the whole of nature as intruding, spying, on him. His terror develops from the first sense that nature has a human identity ("What would it take my standing there for") to a feeling that it is malevolent. The realization of his vulnerability mounts in frantic leaps. Not only is he "in the house alone" but "in [his] life alone," with "no one left but God." The last line is not a cry of faith but an agonized sense of absolute bereavement. The strongly accented "God," only half-rhyming with "abroad," strikes a discordant, unresolved note, and the emotional emphasis remains on "no one."

All the technical elements of the poem assist in this re-creation of remembered terror. The rhyming pattern is narrow (only five rhymes in all) but insistent (the first five lines all rhyme), so that the effect is a relentless, circumscribing pursuit, which is reinforced by the amount of repetition ("Word . . . Word . . . Word"). The introduction of colloquial idioms ("What would it take my standing there for") breaks up any chance of a regular meter, which would create an inappropriate sense of control, and gives a psychological distinctiveness to the voice of the speaker. The poem thus re-creates dramatically a sense of loneliness and terror unusual in the lyric mode.

Not many of Frost's lyrics attempt to re-create an experience of the past; more often they seem to arise out of a present, or at least a recent, observation. "Come In," "Dust of Snow," "Hyla Brook," "The Oven Bird," "Design" do not reach back into the memory for their initial impulse. Yet Frost was as aware as Wordsworth was of the poetic possibilities of emotion recollected in tranquility. In his 1939 preface, "The Figure a Poem Makes," he wrote:

For me the initial delight is in the surprise of remembering something I didn't know I knew. I am in a place, in a situation, as if I had materialized from cloud or risen out of the ground. There is a glad recognition of the long lost and the rest follows. . . . The impressions most useful to my purpose seem always those I was unaware of and so made no note of at the time when taken, and the conclusion is come to [sic] that like giants we are always hurling experience ahead of us to pave the future with against the day when we may want to strike a line of purpose across it for somewhere.[6]

The use of the past as Frost describes it here, however, seems much more accidental and subconscious than in Wordsworth. His poems rarely attempt to impose an order on the past, to see its meaning in terms of the present, or, as Wordsworth's poems often do, to show how the imagination is fed by absorbing the past. In "Bereft" Frost does not try to extract a meaning from this past incident but simply to re-create its terror.

If "Bereft" is intensely personal in subject, "Neither Out Far Nor In Deep" (1934) captures the terror of nihilism in a more objective, low-keyed way. Lionel Trilling claimed that this poem "often seems to me the most perfect poem of our time." In the controversial after-dinner speech that he delivered on Frost's eighty-fifth birthday, he said of it: ". . . see if you are warmed by anything in it except the energy with which emptiness is perceived."[7]

> The people along the sand
> All turn and look one way.
> They turn their back on the land.
> They look at the sea all day.
>
> As long as it takes to pass
> A ship keeps raising its hull;
> The wetter ground like glass
> Reflects a standing gull.
>
> The land may vary more;
> But wherever the truth may be—
> The water comes ashore,
> And the people look at the sea.
>
> They cannot look out far.
> They cannot look in deep.
> But when was that ever a bar
> To any watch they keep?

Trilling was savagely attacked for his astute insight that Frost was a "terrifying poet." But why the outrage at this suggestion? Primarily because Frost had molded his own image as that of the optimistic philosopher who could draw strength from the land itself, and readers were fooled into trusting the teller rather than the tale. But perhaps it was also partly because Frost was adding an unusual dimension to the lyric form. We do not expect lyrics to be "terrifying." They can, of course, be melancholy or elegaic. Traditional lyrics were very often laments, songs of world weariness, of personal loss, and many of Frost's lyrics follow this pattern ("Reluctance," "Desert Places," "Acquainted with the Night").

Such poems as "Design" or "Neither Out Far Nor In Deep," however, have a different perspective. Here the emphasis is not on the speaker's emotion, and the theme is not an individual's sense of alienation from the rest of the world. Here the focus is on the world itself. A door is opened on the possibility that everything is meaningless. It offers a preview of the absurd world of Camus's *The Stranger* and links Frost less with the English lyric poets than with the New England tradition of Hawthorne, Melville, Emily Dickinson, and James, who had all, at some time or other, contemplated the terror of nothingness. The very simplicity of the lyric form here belies the disturbing implications of the meaning.

In "Neither Out Far Nor In Deep" the meter is more regular than in any of the poems we have looked at so far; there is less sense of a speaking voice intruding on the controlled beat. Indeed, one is hardly conscious of a speaker at all. The emphasis is on the scene and its implications, not on the interpreting eye; the element of personality that is so characteristic of the lyric form is markedly absent. The scene is drawn with skilled economy, and, like any good symbolist work, the "meaning" rests in the unstated implications.

The elements of the scene are simple: land, water, and people. Yet it is never, from the opening stanza on, a realistic beach scene; the word "all," mentioned twice in the first four lines, removes any possibility of that. There is something compulsive about these people and the watch they keep. Pictorially, it has something of the quality of the Norwegian Expressionist, Edvard Munch—stylized, desolate, the people unindividualized and static like a tragic chorus, their faces unidentified, their eyes blurred. The focus of the poem's attention is in their gazing, and the significance of that rests both in what they are turning away from and what they are looking at.

The juxtaposition of land and sea to suggest metaphoric values has a long literary tradition. Perhaps the best example of it in American literature is *Moby Dick*. There the land represents order, security, human values, harmony. By contrast, the sea is unknowable, inscrutable, alluring, and destructive. It represents the "insistent question" to all those who cannot be content with the complacent security of their landlocked existences. Ishmael feels drawn to the sea whenever he feels "a damp, drizzly November in [his] soul," and the sea's attraction for him throws light on Frost's poem:

Why did the old Persians hold the sea holy? Why did the Greeks give it a separate deity, and own brother of Jove? Surely all this is not without meaning. And still deeper the meaning of that story of Narcissus, who because he could not grasp the tormenting, mild image he saw in the fountain, plunged into it and was drowned. But that same image, we ourselves see in all rivers and oceans. It is the image of the ungraspable phantom of life; and this is the key to it all.

But in "Neither Out Far Nor In Deep" there is
an ironic twist. The "people" don't go to sea, as
Ishmael does; they simply look at it, hypnotized into a
state of inertia. All that there is to see is contained in
stanza 2—a ship, mechanically passing to an unstated
destination, and a gull, viewed only as a reflection—
and there is no assurance that the "people" even see
that. Their gaze is obsessive, which is emphasized by
the repetition of "look" throughout the poem. Yet
they gaze on emptiness. They "turn their back on the
land," which "may vary more," compelled into an
abstract contemplation of blankness:

> They cannot look out far.
> They cannot look in deep.

There is nothing in the poem to meet their "insistent
question" as there was in *Moby Dick*. If there were, we
could interpret the final stanza as a tribute to man's
indomitable or insatiable spirit. But their waiting is
eternal and hopeless.

The theme of the poem is thus held in a subtle
balance. Is it a commentary on the tragic limitations
of man's perception? Or does it go further than that
to postulate a blank and absurd universe that mocks
the very attempt to "look"? The ambiguity is unresolved, the poem ends in a question. But it is a question that is indeed "terrifying" in its possibilities. The
brilliant word choice of the final line maintains the
ambiguity: "To any watch they keep." The image of
"keeping watch" suggests a fear of something real,
though unseeable; but it could also suggest as futile a
vigil as that of the tramps in *Waiting for Godot*.

If Frost in "Neither Out Far Nor In Deep" ex-
panded the dimensions of the lyric poem by develop-

ing a more objective and symbolic mode, in "The Hill Wife" (1916) he moved the frontier further to accommodate the psychological and dramatic. "The Hill Wife," in fact, is closer in concept to such dramatic narratives as "A Servant to Servants" or "The Fear." Yet in form it retains the rhyme and stanzaic patterning, and the focus on a persona, that we associate with the lyric.

The poem is divided into five shorter poems ("Loneliness," "House Fear," "The Smile," "The Oft-Repeated Dream," and "The Impulse"), written separately over a span of eight years. Each is a tableau, revealing a separate facet of one woman's mind, a psychological milestone in her disintegration into insanity. Two poems in the cycle feature the wife as speaker; the other three are presented by an omniscient narrator, sitting as it were off stage and giving us the detached perspective that the characters themselves are incapable of.

Frost was always interested in problems of mental instability, and the characters of his poems often dramatize the abrasiveness or insensitivity of human relationships. In "The Hill Wife," for instance, the husband does not appear until the last poem, but his very absence in the first four poems, as the woman's hold on reality gets weaker, is significant. His neglect must take a share of the blame for her collapse.

"Loneliness," subtitled "Her Word," is a dramatic monologue spoken by the wife. We need to hear it as a psychoanalyst would hear it, noting her preoccupations and the language she chooses to express them. At this stage her speech is fairly structured and controlled; the twelve lines are shaped into three stanzas and the meter is reasonably regular.

> One ought not to have to care
>> So much as you and I
> Care when the birds come round the house
>> To seem to say good-by;
>
> Or care so much when they come back
>> With whatever it is they sing;
> The truth being we are as much
>> Too glad for the one thing
>
> As we are too sad for the other here—
>> With birds that fill their breasts
> But with each other and themselves
>> And their built or driven nests.

There is perhaps too much formality, too little spontaneity, in her opening stanza. But in her manner of speaking we have no hint of mental or emotional instability. She can still, moreover, identify with her husband. Yet even in this slight tableau there are a few puzzles. Why is she so introspectively concerned about "caring"? Why is their caring seen as excessive ("too glad" or "too sad")? Why is she projecting human emotions onto the birds ("that fill their breasts / But with each other and themselves")?

In "House Fear," which is the second poem in this little drama, the curtain opens, as it were, on a narrator, an external commentator on the action. In his ten perfectly controlled and objective lines, he simply recounts an odd habit that the couple have. Whenever they return at night to their lonely farmhouse,

> They learned to rattle the lock and key
> To give whatever might chance to be,
> Warning and time to be off in flight.

We are not told who is afraid here—the man or his wife. The narrator simply presents it as an action they are united on.

But by the third poem, "The Smile," another dramatic monologue voiced by the woman, the sense of persecution is definitely hers. This tableau enacts one of Frost's personal terrors—the visit of an unknown tramp to a lonely homestead. In this twelve-line poem, the wife worries about the smile on the face of a tramp to whom they have just given some bread—a smile that "never came of being gay." For the first time we see her tense neuroticism. Her paranoia rises quickly in the series of speculations she makes about the incident. "Perhaps" he smiled out of pity for their poverty in being able to give only bread, "perhaps" out of a smug superiority in letting "us give instead / Of seizing from us," or, finally, "perhaps" out of mockery

> at us for being wed,
> Or being very young (and he was pleased
> To have a vision of us old and dead).

That last "perhaps" is a quite irrational leap, reflecting the woman's frantic imbalance. Her last line—"He's watching from the woods as like as not"—is a classic statement of paranoia.

The mental separation of husband and wife is quite clear in the fourth poem, "The Oft-Repeated Dream." The dream—of which "only one of the two / Was afraid"—is of a great dark pine tree and what it "might do" if it could intrude into the bedroom. As in "Bereft," a psychological terror makes the natural world anthropomorphic: the tree has "tireless but ineffectual hands" that are "forever trying the window

latch." And, although the dream is oft-repeated, the
woman is now unable even to articulate her fear. She
"had no saying dark enough / For the dark pine."
Without even the ability to control experience
through language, she is a prey to absolute disintegration.

The disintegration occurs in the last poem of the
series, "The Impulse." The first three stanzas reiterate
her loneliness as, childless, she followed her husband
plowing or sat on a log singing "to herself." And then
one day—as simply and undramatically as the mind
breaks—she "strayed" out of his life.

> Sudden and swift and light as that
>   The ties gave,
> And he learned of finalities
>   Besides the grave.

If the set of poems that makes up this little drama
demonstrates one of the directions in which Frost
extended the mode of the dramatic lyric, the extraordinary poem "The Subverted Flower" (1942) demonstrates another. Again the drama centers on the
relationship between a man and a woman, but here
the psychological tensions are captured in a single
scene and the drama begins, classically, *in medias res.*
The theme is an unusual one in Frost—a man's sexual
advances to a girl who is frightened and repelled by
them. What is even more unusual is that Frost ap-
parently wrote it as early as 1913. He told Lawrance
Thompson that he could have included it in *A Boy's
Will*,[8] where it would certainly have stood out in
sharp contrast to the fairly traditional lyrics of that
volume. But Mrs. Frost would never allow it to be
published in her lifetime—a censorship that may

simply reflect a general Victorian prudishness against the explicitness of the subject but, more likely, hints at a certain autobiographical basis to this poem.

What is extraordinary about "The Subverted Flower" is not only the force of the startling imagery, but the psychological exactness with which the action is presented. The scene is pastoral—the girl is "standing to the waist / In goldenrod and brake," and the reader expects the human relationship to be correspondingly idyllic. Indeed, the man's sexuality is seen first in flower imagery—something natural and beautiful, but also transient and vulnerable, "tender-headed." His smile is shy and encouraging. But the girl's reaction, whether out of ignorance or positive unkindness, "subverts" the flower, and the imagery relating to the man changes dramatically from that of flowers to that of bestiality. Under the girl's interpretation of his advances, his "smile" of encouragement becomes "another sort of smile" cracking a "ragged muzzle." His lips become "sucked and blown" as his words make him "choke / Like a tiger at a bone." She "dared not stir a foot" for fear "movement should provoke / The demon of pursuit / That slumbers in a brute." So far the psychological projections, of terror and disgust, have been the girl's. But at her mother's call "from inside the garden wall," a humiliating self-consciousness overcomes the man and the sense of shame and disgust transfers itself to him:

> A hand hung like a paw,
> An arm worked like a saw
> As if to be persuasive,
> An ingratiating laugh
> That cut the snout in half,
> An eye become evasive.

The man turns and runs, "obeying bestial laws, /
A coward save at night," and she hears him "bark
outright" in the distance. At the end, because psychological projections always throw a light backward as
well as forward, the animal imagery is extended to in-
clude the girl, too. The "bitter words she spit" after the
stumbling, retreating "dog or what it was" make her
mother wipe "the foam / From her chin" and draw
her "backward home." The "backward" is loaded; she
is like one of Blake's innocents, rejecting the possibilities of experience and retreating back to childhood
securities.

Any moral judgment in the poem is subdued and
incidental:

> A girl could only see
> That a flower had marred a man,
> But what she could not see
> Was that the flower might be
> Other than base and fetid:
> That the flower had done but part,
> And what the flower began
> Her own too meager heart
> Had terribly completed.

More forcefully, the poem dramatizes shame as a product of human consciousness and manages to hold in a
delicate balance both the man's and the girl's points
of view. The ending is harrowing precisely because
there has been no resolution. Unusual in its conception and consummate in its craftsmanship, "The Subverted Flower" is one of Frost's most brilliant lyrics.
The wonder is that it has been underrated for so long.

A final example of Frost's variations of tone and
subject within a predominantly lyric form may be
found in the cynical "Provide, Provide" (1934). It is

Frost's most sarcastic poem, in which all the traditional techniques of rhyme and meter are used to undercut the apparent theme.

The poem begins with a nursery-rhyme lilt that introduces the story of "Abishag" as a kind of mid-Victorian cautionary tale:

> The witch that came (the withered hag)
> To wash the steps with pail and rag
> Was once the beauty Abishag.

It is the American rags-to-riches story in reverse. And who better to enact a cautionary tale than this "picture pride of Hollywood" with her memory of having "starred"? The biblical name Abishag was obviously chosen for the comic effect of the rhyme, but it is not entirely without thematic relevance. She is the namesake of the young woman, "exceedingly beautiful," who was called in to stir the passions of the dying King David. They are both, in the language of women's lib, "sexual objects." Our Abishag's identity is simply a celluloid creation, a factitious product of that least real of all worlds, Hollywood. As "the picture pride of Hollywood," she is a peculiarly twentieth-century extension of the American Dream, full of glitter without substance, fame without identity.

The voice that intones this cautionary tale seems, as we might expect, earnest, dogmatic, self-righteous. Yet, even in that opening stanza, there are clear indications that the voice is parodying itself and its attitudes. The cloak-and-dagger effect of the parentheses in the first line, the pat rhyme scheme, the Cinderella cliché of "pail and rag," and especially the choice of that outlandish biblical name, all pre-

pare us for a farcical reversal of the expected moral
values. And indeed the stated "moral" of the tale is
not quite so mid-Victorian as the verse form:

> Die early and avoid the fate.
> Or if predestined to die late,
> Make up your mind to die in state.
>
> . . . .
>
> Some have relied on what they knew,
> Others on being simply true.
> What worked for them might work for you.

By the ending, the nursery-rhyme lilt has given way to
oracular pronouncement.

> Better to go down dignified
> With boughten friendship at your side
> Than none at all. Provide, provide!

The satiric thrust is at some of the most sacred
cows in the American value scheme: at materialism
("Provide, Provide!"); at pragmatism ("What worked
for them might work for you"); and at the good old
republican conviction that success will come to those
who set about it with vigor ("Make up your mind to
die in state"). The odd thing is that the latter two
were generally among Frost's own sacred cows.

In "Provide, Provide!" the double-edged ironies
that give the poem its force are largely created by the
speaker's highly conscious manipulation of conventional lyric techniques. The triteness of the unsubtle
meter forms a fitting vehicle for the triteness of the
stated moral; and the simplistic value scheme is re-
soundingly mocked by the simplistic rhyme scheme.

The lyric voice was Frost's first voice, the pre-
dominant genre of *A Boy's Will.* The voice of his

later dramatic narratives might perhaps seem more distinctively Frost's, might seem to accord more with his theorizing about poetry, but Frost maintained his interest in the lyric all his life. That he did so suggests he saw no discrepancy between the demands of the lyric form and the need to create the sounds of the speaking voice. "Tune" remained as important to him as to the most traditional lyricist singing to the accompaniment of his lyre. Frost simply enlarged the definition of the word.

3

•••

The Dramatic
Narrative

Everything written is as good as it is dramatic.
—preface to "The Constant Symbol"

From the earliest attempts that Frost made at articulating his poetic intentions, the one element that took precedence over all others was sound. "Sound" in poetry had almost magical qualities; it was the element "but for which imagination would become reason." Yet, as we have seen, he tried to distinguish his concept of poetic sound from the prevailing musicality of much *fin de siècle* poetry. He often told the story of how his theory of sound was crystallized for him. A clergyman friend, reading some of Frost's very early poems, complained that they were "too near the level of talk." That was it! "Talk" was precisely the effect he wanted. A master conversationalist, he had often wondered why it was so much easier to create "living sentences" when talking to a friend than when trying to write:

Why was a friend so much more effective than a piece of paper in drawing the living sentences out of me? I thought it might come to my having to remember exactly the shape my sentences took under provocation or under social excitement. How would a piece of paper ever get the best out of me? I was afraid I hadn't imagination enough to be really literary. And I hadn't. I have just barely enough to imitate spoken sentences.[1]

The answer, then, was to re-create in writing the impression of a speaking voice.

But where does meaning come from in talk? Obviously it does not come simply from the fixed denotations, the dictionary meaning, of the words themselves. Frost often cited the extreme situation of listening to the sounds of voices behind a closed door, where individual words could not be distinguished at all, yet where the "meaning" could largely be gained from the abstract sound of the rise and fall of the voices, angry or soothing, excited or perfunctory. It is the tone of the living voice that helps to create the meaning of any utterance. As another example of abstract sound, of meaning derived purely from tone of voice, Frost wrote, in 1913, in a letter to John Bartlett:

Ask yourself how these sentences would sound without the words in which they are embodied:

> You mean to tell me you can't read?
> I said no such thing.
> Well read then.
> You're not my teacher.[2]

Presumably if we heard these sentences from behind closed doors—"without the words," as it were—we would still have some idea of the interchange, simply from the tones of voice that the sentences so clearly imply: the first surprised, the second indignant, and so on.

What Frost was trying to understand through such an exercise was "the abstract vitality of our speech," what he called "pure sound—pure form." But the full vitality of language, he would claim, comes from a bringing-together of the words, with their fixed denotative meaning, and the tone of voice in which they are said, which can extend, modify, or even contradict (as in irony) that meaning. This bringing-together Frost called "the sound of sense," and he aimed at re-creating this in his poetry. His appeal would be to an "audial imagination" rather than a visual one, an imagination that was sensitive to the nuances of spoken tones. The reader must be left in no doubt as to how to say any sentence in a poem. So Frost concentrated on establishing a dramatic context within each poem that would determine its intonational quality. He was quoted in an interview as saying:

I try to make each word serve two purposes; in addition to its own meaning it serves as a guide to the voice in reading preceding and surrounding words. If this is not always true of each word, it is true of each phrase or line.[3]

A good poem, then, is something of a performance, not only by the writer but by the reader also. The reader must assume what Frost called the right "sound posture" or "vocal gesture" in order to understand the poem fully; he must assume the role of the poem's persona. For this reason the tone must be something within his own experience, something that he can recognize. "I say you can't read a single good sentence with the salt in it unless you have previously heard it spoken," Frost claimed.

The living part of a poem is the intonation entangled somehow in the syntax idiom and meaning of a sentence. It is only there for those who have heard it previously in conversation. It is not for us in any Greek or Latin poem because our ears have not been filled with the tones of Greek and Roman talk. It is the most volatile and at the same time important part of poetry. It goes and the language becomes a dead language, the poetry dead poetry.[4]

By thus concentrating his attention on capturing tones of voice in his poetry, Frost was asserting the extraordinary flexibility of a naturally accentual language like English. In Latin poetry, every syllable was a fixed quantity, short or long—and that, Frost would say, was the Romans' loss. When the English poet laureate Robert Bridges tried to apply the same

principle to English prosody—asserting that all sylla-
bles in English have an absolute and measurable
quantity regardless of their context—Frost rightly
hooted in derision. Of course the sound of any word
alters according to its syntax and its tone. As he wrote
to Sidney Cox, talking of Bridges: "I will find you the
word 'come' variously used in various passages as a
whole, half, third, fourth, fifth, and sixth note. It is as
long as the sense makes it."[5]

And what about the "meaning" of pauses and
silences, which Bridges was ignoring? Frost took
pride in the way the context changed the tone of
each of the four "don'ts" in his "Home Burial," and
the way the voice controlled the pace of the threatening "If—you—do!" at the end of that poem.

Frost's insistence on establishing a dramatic
context ("sound posture," "vocal gesture") in a poem
indicates the closeness of his poetry to drama. He
was dogmatic on this point: "Everything written is
as good as it is dramatic. It need not declare itself
in form but it is drama or nothing."[6] In fact, he
wrote only three plays as plays, but the stage adap-
tation of several of his narrative poems gives testimony to their essentially dramatic conception. "The
Death of the Hired Man," "Home Burial," and
"Snow" were all performed on the stage. The source
of any dramatic interest, he insisted, must be in the
language itself and the vocal posture needed to speak
it. He scorned elaborate stage directions in a play because they lessened this function of language. Thus, in
a letter to Edwin Arlington Robinson in 1915, Frost
praised Robinson's play *The Porcupine* for the way
the dialogue is made to carry so much dramatic
weight:

It is good writing, or better than that, good speaking caught
alive—every sentence of it. The speaking tones are all there
on the printed page, nothing is left for the actor but to
recognize and give them. And the action is in the speech
where it should be, and not along beside it in antics for the
body to perform. I wonder if you agree with me that the
best sentences are those that convey their own tone—that
haven't to be described in italics. "With feline demureness"
for instance is well imagined as it is, but do you suppose it
wouldnt have been possible to make the sentence to follow
indicate in itself the vocal posture you had in mind.[7]

Most of the poems of *A Boy's Will* were lyrics.
And although, as we have seen, they were given a
certain dramatic quality through the personas of the
individual poems, it was not until his second volume,
North of Boston, published in the following year
(1914), that Frost found his real dramatic voice.

This is not to say, of course, that these first volumes mark the limits of Frost's lyric and dramatic
poetry respectively. Both genres were to remain
among his most popular in later work. But, as separate volumes, *A Boy's Will* and *North of Boston* do
have a unity about them that is not common to any
of Frost's later books. It is as if within these two
distinctive voices—the one so aware of "tune" and
cadence, and the other so alive to the dramatic
possibilities of ordinary speech intonations—Frost
found all the ingredients he needed to blend his own
individual poetic voice.

At the time when the dramatic narratives of
North of Boston were first published, Frost confused
the issue somewhat by calling them "dramatic eclogues," after the eclogues of Theocritus and Virgil.
The classical eclogue described an idyllic pastoral

scene, with rustic characters conversing in "dramatic" dialogue that was fairly stylized. Frost's poems are generally starker. They are "pastoral" only insofar as they are set in rural New England. Writing from as far away as old England, he was homesick for his own country, north of Boston; and the features of the New England landscape—with its stone walls, apple orchards, wooden barns, birch trees, and sharply defined seasons—provide a fully realized yet unintrusive backdrop to the human dramas of Frost's "eclogues." Yet the poems are rarely idyllic, and the characters have little connection with the stylized shepherds of Theocritus. They are lonely, tragic, stoic, often psychologically disturbed, with a tough pragmatism and a laconic humor as their only defenses against the harshness of their lives. Yet Frost knew and loved these Yankee farmers and the nostalgia of distance heightened his response to them as well as to the landscape. In 1913, when he was gathering the poems for *North of Boston*, he wrote to the English poet F. S. Flint:

Did I give you a feeling of and for the independent-dependence of the kind of people I like to write about. I am no propagandist of equality. But I enjoy above all things the contemplation of equality when it happily exists. I am no snob. . . . The John Kline* who lost his housekeeper and went down like a felled ox was just the person I have described and I never knew a man I liked better—damn the world anyway.[8]

 * Frost is referring to his poem "The Housekeeper," a story based on the actual experience of a New England neighbor, John Hall, whose name is used in the poem. Frost is here momentarily confusing him with another neighbor, John Kline.

Frost's respect for the independent-dependence of such people was strong, though it would seem to have been easily misread. When the poet Amy Lowell announced once that she was leaving New Hampshire, Frost asked her why. She couldn't stand the people, she replied. What's wrong with the people, Frost countered. "Read your own books and find out," she snapped. But a close reading of Frost's books would never disclose his characters in such a negative light. The psychology of these "eclogues" is as subtle as the verse form—the capturing of the sound of sense—is sophisticated.

Although it does Frost no service to categorize his poems too strictly, it may be useful in examining his dramatic narratives to separate them into three broad categories. There are, first of all, the "static" dramas—usually just one scene, described by an objective narrator—in which all the dramatic implications are inherent in the visual effect, rather than in dialogue or action. "An Old Man's Winter Night," "Meeting and Passing," "Two Look at Two," and even "The Most of It" are examples of such understated, undeveloped "dramas." Secondly, there are the dramatic monologues such as "A Servant to Servants" or "The Pauper Witch of Grafton," in which the single speaker takes the center of the stage, and the spotlight is wholly on her life story and her character. Finally, there are the more obvious "dramas"—"The Death of the Hired Man," "Home Burial," "The Fear"—which present the interaction of several characters, several voices.

The work of such European writers as Chekhov, Turgenev, and Maeterlinck had brought a new dimension to the art of storytelling, and Frost was certainly familiar with at least the latter two. He once claimed, in fact, that "some things in Turgenieff must have had a good deal to do with the making of me."[9] For these writers, conflict was no longer the essence of drama. Since much of life is uneventful, the depiction of an uneventful life could convey intimations of the spiritual reality that transcends mere physical reality. Nor did dialogue have to be used to advance the action of the plot; Chekhov's characters generally talk at, rather than to, each other, and the effect of an unbridgeable emptiness in their lives is devastating. A static scene could be the concentrated essence of all the drama that ever was.

Maeterlinck once described as supreme drama the immobile presentation of an old man sitting at night in his armchair with a lamp beside him and "giving unconscious ear to all the eternal laws that reign about his house, interpreting, without comprehending, the silence of doors and windows and the quivering voice of the light, submitting with bent head to the presence of his soul and his destiny." Such a man, he claimed, transfixes for the viewer "a deeper, more human and more universal life" than the more usual run of dramatic characters—"the lover who strangles his mistress, the captain who conquers in battle, or the husband who avenges his honor."[10] The presentation of such a static scene has a dramatic quality similar to some of Rembrandt's portraits in which a shaft of light, like an authorial directive, focuses our attention on the simple tilt of a head, or the expressive lines of a face, or a revealing gesture frozen in time. "It is a poem just to mention driving into a strange barn to bide the pass-

ing of a thunder storm,"[11] Frost wrote to a friend
in 1915, thus confirming the appeal that static drama
held for him.

The ingredients of the scene Maeterlinck described are all present in Frost's "An Old Man's
Winter Night," published in his third volume,
Mountain Interval (1916). Here the action is simple
—an old man, wandering alone in an empty house
on a winter night, finally goes to sleep beside the
stove. Yet each item in the scene takes on a significance that is archetypal, almost symbolic, so that
the poem goes further than simply capturing the
loneliness and pathos of old age and presents a
profound opposition of life against death, light
against dark, order against chaos. Each ingredient
in this concentrated drama—the setting, the human
actions, the sound effects—embodies a subdued dramatic tension. In the end nothing is resolved, and to
impose any single "meaning" on the poem is to deny
the deliberate resonance of Frost's dramatic technique.

On one level, it is tempting to view the poem, as
some critics have done, simply as a study of death,
or at least of human inadequacy. The emphasis from
the opening lines on is certainly on the darkness and
vastness of the night outside, pressing in on the
house:

> All out-of-doors looked darkly in at him
> Through the thin frost, almost in separate stars,
> That gathers on the pane in empty rooms.

The animistic natural world, which reminds us of
"Bereft," seems foreboding. The lamp that the old
man holds up prevents him from seeing anything of

this great "out-of-doors." Besides suggesting the
limitations of human vision, this detail gives him all
the vulnerability of anyone who stands in a pool of
light and cannot see outside of it.

> What kept his eyes from giving back the gaze
> Was the lamp tilted near them in his hand.
> What kept him from remembering what it was
> That brought him to that creaking room was age.

The old man forgets what he came into the room
for, and his aimless "clomping," sounding like "beat-
ing on a box," may epitomize the futility of any
existence that leads so inevitably to this coffinlike
state. He sits down, consigns his world to the moon
to "keep"—and sleeps so deeply that not even the
sound of a log shifting in the stove could disturb
him. Is this the sleep that our little lives are rounded
with? Is it the same dreamlike sleep as in "After
Apple Picking"? If so, the total picture does indeed
seem negative, ending not with a bang but a whim-
per.

> One aged man—one man—can't keep a house,
> A farm, a countryside, or if he can,
> It's thus he does it of a winter night.

Such a reading seems reasonably coherent. Yet
for every detail that suggests simply a failure of the
old man's consciousness, there is an answering one
that suggests assertion. Both the sounds and the
lighting of this static drama work on contrast, and
the contrasts, as in any good drama, are thematically
significant. There are, for example, three kinds of
light in the poem—the pale light of the moon, the
lamp that the old man carries, and the more spiritual
"light" that "he was to no one but himself." Each

has its limitations, yet together they balance one another dramatically and extend the thematic implications of the poem. The moonlight, "such as she was,"
does little to alleviate the overwhelming darkness of
the natural world outside; but to it the old man
consigns "his snow upon the roof / His icicles along
the wall to keep." That simple idiomatic word "keep"
is repeated four lines later, this time in reference
to the old man: "One aged man . . . can't keep a
house, / A farm, a countryside, or if he can, / It's
thus he does it of a winter night." Its meaning, so
deliberately tied up with local idiom, is vague: keep
watch over? protect? control? Whatever it means its
repetition links the moonlight to the old man's personal light: both are guardians, inadequate perhaps,
yet persistent. Each balances the other; even the
qualifying phrase "such as she was" is balanced and
answered by the later, more positive qualifying
phrase "or if he can." The human "light" is holding
its own, even when it appears to have gone out. The
lamplight is simply mechanical, necessary in the
house but ultimately limiting the vision, and it acts
as a foil for the other two lights.

Similarly, human and natural sounds are juxta-
posed, and again we see the human holding its own.
The sounds of the outer night are "familiar," coming
from "common things," like "the roar of trees and
crack of branches"; yet the outer night is "scared"
by the less familiar sounds of the old man's "clomping."

But more than anything else it is the voice of
this poem that controls our response to the situation
and prevents us from seeing it as a one-dimensional
study of old age and death. If the visual scene has

pathos in it, the voice that presents it has none. What the voice brings out is not the poignancy but the self-containedness of the old man. There is no self-pity in it—rather a quietly assertive independence that answers the darkness of the winter night that he cannot see into:

> A light he was to no one but himself
> Where now he sat, concerned with he knew what.

He nonchalantly "consigned to the moon" those imprisoning forces of the out-of-doors, "his snow upon the roof / His icicles along the wall"; yet the mention that they are "his" snow and "his" icicles, as well as the sense of ownership and control implied in the word "consigned," reassures us that the extinction of his light in sleep is not a defeat. His sleep is a positive action, and if we still needed to be convinced of this, the rhythm picks up the resoluteness of the voice, throwing the emphasis on the action by placing it at the beginning of a line and making it almost a separate sentence:

> He consigned to the moon . . .
>
> . . . .
>
> His icicles along the wall to keep;
> And slept.

All through the poem the voice has been pragmatic, laconic, positive. It expresses a refusal to be bluffed by metaphysical forces. Even in the explanation of the seeming helplessness of the old man, it argues in terms of accountable realities: "what kept him" from seeing outside was the lamp, "what kept him" from remembering what he'd "clomped" into the room for was age. The explanations are simple and not at all pathetic. Even the word "clomping" has a half-humorous assertiveness about it, and in the old man's weighing-up of the "broken moon" as custodian of his snow and icicles—"better than the sun in any case / For such a charge"—there is the witty shrewdness of the Yankee trader.

The old man is certainly not defeated. But to say that he triumphs because, like Faulkner's characters, he endures is not quite true either. The whole conversational flexibility of the voice that presents the drama to us works against taking him so seriously. Rather, he is like that wily pragmatic character in a later poem, "A Drumlin Woodchuck." There is a time for attack and a time for retreat, a time for coping with the dark forces of nature and a time for quietly husbanding one's resources. The old man's sleep is neither more nor less than that. Dramatically, Frost has presented a single scene, has invested it with several emotional possibilities, and has resolved it in a delicate balance of pathos and humor, defeat and undefeatability, that is characteristically his own.

Another such static drama, less profound yet equally delicate and understated, is "Meeting and Passing" (1916). Again the "action," as in Turgenev or Chekhov, is so simple as to be almost nonexistent. The speaker of the poem, on a walk down a hill on a country road, stops to look at the view. As he turns to resume his walk, he sees a woman coming up the hill. They meet and talk:

> We met. But all
> We did that day was mingle great and small
> Footprints in summer dust as if we drew
> The figure of our being less than two

> But more than one as yet. Your parasol
> Pointed the decimal off with one deep thrust.

Afterward they each go their separate ways. That is all. Yet the scene has all the implicit drama of a mime.

In its essentially visual quality, this poem is as close to the Imagist movement as Frost ever came. It centers on one scene, one "image," unemotionally described. Although it has a persona, the speaking voice here is less clearly characterized than in "An Old Man's Winter Night." It is not the voice but the scene itself that controls the dramatic response here. The effect is like looking at a silent film.

"Meeting and Passing" is a love story, and it captures all the delicate hesitations, the tentative attraction, the shy responsiveness, and the private sense of communion of any love in its early stages. Yet there is not a single "emotional" phrase in the poem; it is all achieved by gesture and statement. "We met." Just that. The statement does not even break up the meter of the line, though the fact that it is a separate sentence adds weight to its sparse simplicity. The "narrative," such as it is, pauses, and, as in a film, the focus closes in on a single image—the "summer dust" and the hieroglyphics there that chart so subtly the course of this relationship. There the mingling of large and small footprints, being "all [they] did that day," acts as a testimony of their communion and their separation from anything else, so that even the speaker can see the metaphor there—"as if we drew / The figure of our being less than two / But more than one as yet." And, as the girl talks to him, smiling privately in her shy self-consciousness and poking at the ground with her parasol, he whimsically sees that mark of the parasol as being the "decimal" point of the love that is "less than two / But more than one as yet." Their total union might eventually obviate the necessity for such a self-conscious gesture, however appealing it may be. The last two lines capture love's delighted sense of a merging of identity, with all the reticence that this love has expressed itself in:

> Afterward I went past what you had passed
> Before we met, and you what I had passed.

Through the appropriately clumsy expression in these lines we sense the additional charm, barely finding articulation, that the landscape now has for them both as each walks in the other's footsteps.

Frost's dramatic monologues are more obviously "dramatic" than such visual presentations as "An Old Man's Winter Night" and "Meeting and Passing," where the dramatic tensions are wholly implicit. Frost admitted to being influenced by Browning. In any case, his own emphasis on capturing tones of voice and creating a dramatic context to make such tones obvious, would direct him naturally toward the form of the dramatic monologue. Yet in fact he wrote comparatively few poems that are strictly in this mode.

Perhaps his best dramatic monologue is the haunting "A Servant to Servants," published in *North of Boston* (1914). Like Browning, Frost was interested in abnormal psychology, and his narratives are filled with examples of eccentric, even macabre, human behavior. His characters tend to be lonely, neurotic figures haunted by their past, with nowhere to go in the present. It was not literary precedent alone that directed him in such interests. More personal factors lay behind his choice of character and subject. One was that Frost wrote of the rural settings he knew, and rural communities generally tend to throw into relief eccentric characters and actions. Even the most fanciful of Frost's narratives have some basis in "realism"; they are generally based on something he experienced or heard. But, apart from this concern for the realism of his characters, Frost himself had trodden close enough to the borderline of insanity to be fascinated by the more erratic twistings of the human mind.

The background of "A Servant to Servants" goes back to the summer of 1900. In one of his regular escapes from the misery of summer hayfever, from which he suffered all his life, Frost took his family on a camping holiday by the shores of Lake Willoughby in Vermont. He was interested in botany at the time, and the area offered great varieties of ferns and flowers. They camped in a pasture owned by a Mr. Connelley, and Frost often talked to Mrs. Connelley as he bought milk and eggs. A pathetically tired woman, overworked, fearful of hereditary insanity, Mrs. Connelley loved the chance to talk to a sympathetic listener. The woman in "A Servant to Servants" is primarily based on her character and story.

In the monologue the woman is talking—somewhat compulsively, since the poem is one hundred and seventy-seven lines long—to a summer camper. As in any dramatic monologue, she is characterized not only by the subjects she talks about but by her choice of words, her phrasing, her recurring preoccupations, her generalizations, and by her sudden silences and breakings-off. She begins by telling the camper how glad she is to have him camp on their land, though within five lines she has broached the subject that is to run as a leitmotif all through the poem—her constant tiredness, "with a houseful of hungry men to feed." Yet her self-preoccupation is never self-pity. Indeed, there is a sense of detachment—psychologically more disturbing perhaps—toward herself. She breaks off midsentence, a mannerism itself indicating an inability to cope with the problem. She blames a failure of expression—"I can't express my feelings"—but is aware that the failure goes deeper:

> There's nothing but a voice-like left inside
> That seems to tell me how I ought to feel,
> And would feel if I wasn't all gone wrong.

With extraordinary economy and dramatic sureness, Frost in the first fifteen lines has presented the basic elements of his drama: a woman, overworked and overtired, glad of even the transient company of the camper, only half-articulate, doubting the reality of her emotions to the point where she feels devoid of all emotions. The symptoms of mild schizophrenia are there.

Abruptly she changes the subject to Lake Willoughby. Even here, through the conversational politeness ("And you like it here?" "How did you hear of it?"), there is evidence of tension. She describes how, to take her mind "off doughnuts and soda biscuit," she likes to step outside the kitchen and "take the water dazzle" on a sunny day or "take the rising wind" when a storm threatens. That perhaps is normal enough, though it is a lonely gesture.

But why is she so intent on rationalizing the advantages of the lake?

> I look and look at it.
> I see it's a fair, pretty sheet of water.
> I stand and make myself repeat out loud
> The advantages it has. . . .

Later changes of subject are less abrupt and suggest not so much a neurotic fragmentation of mind as a desperate anxiousness to hold on to realities, to the normalities of human behavior—their business prospects, her husband's work, their reasons for coming to the lake. Yet her anxieties and resentments come through; she can barely cope with her situation. There is a temperamental distance between her husband, Len, and herself that gives a clue to her sense of isolation. Len is the archetypal Yankee, pragmatic and self-reliant ("He looks on the bright side of everything / Including me"; "He says the best way out is always through"; "He's into everything in town"). But he is also insensitive, like the husband in "The Hill Wife," to his wife's incipient breakdown ("He thinks I'll be all right / With doctoring"). She barely admits her resentment, but it is there:

> By good rights I ought not to have so much
> Put on me, but there seems no other way.

Len's work—though she admits that "he works when he works as hard as I do" and that in any case "there's small profit in comparisons"—is after all only a man's work, "from sun to sun," and free from the grind of "doing / Things over and over that just won't stay done." He can escape into town; he

can fill the house with boarders who only add to her
strain, increase her sense of depersonalization ("No
more put out in what they do or say / Than if I
wasn't in the room at all"), and raise a new kind of
fear ("whether they are safe / To have inside the
house with doors unlocked").

It is only after voicing such resentment that she
gives the most revelatory glimpse of her own background: "I have my fancies; it runs in the family."
She admits that she has "been away once" in the
state asylum, and goes on to narrate the story of her
insane uncle who lived in the house where she was
brought up. It is a tale of unmitigated horror: the
uncle lived in a "sort of cage" upstairs, with straw to
lie on ("Anything they put in for furniture / He'd
tear to pieces"); he was fed "without dishes," naked,
often screaming in the night, wearing the bars of his
cage smooth from pulling them apart. With such a
background we begin to piece together all the
woman's hints of loneliness, fear, drudgery, and
purposelessness. The move to the lake seemed an
escape:

> . . . I looked to be happy, and I was,
> As I said, for a while—but I don't know!
> Somehow the change wore out like a prescription.

From a sickness that is soul deep, there can be no
simple escape:

> . . . there's more to it than just window views
> And living by a lake. I'm past such help—

The story is an intensely moving one. The
woman embodies that "independent-dependence" that
Frost respected so much in his characters. The psy-

chological observation is astute, but what really distinguishes this poem as a dramatic monologue is the extraordinary flexibility of the blank verse. It exemplifies clearly what Frost meant by the "sound of sense." Apply his own test to almost any line; imagine what the sentence would sound like without the words, with just the abstract intonation as if we were listening from behind closed doors:

> Our Willoughby! How did you hear of it?
> I expect, though, everyone's heard of it.
> In a book about ferns? Listen to that!
> You let things more like feathers regulate
> Your going and coming.

Or at the end of the poem:

> Bless you, of course you're keeping me from work,
> But the thing of it is, I need to *be* kept.
> There's work enough to do—there's always that;
> But behind's behind. The worst that you can do
> Is set me back a little more behind.

It is the "voice posture" that gives life to these lines. The dramatic situation determines exactly the way they must be said; we could almost graph the woman's facial expressions by their intonation. They are indeed "spoken sounds, caught fresh," and they play a large part in establishing the psychological realism of this monologue. From them, too, we realize what Frost meant when he claimed that intonation is "only there for those who have heard it previously in conversation." This poem, because so much of the "meaning" resides in the subtle intonations of the spoken voice, is virtually untranslatable. That may be true of most dramatic monologues, but it is particularly true of Frost's.

In "The Pauper Witch of Grafton" (1921), the intonations are more humorous, and the psychological study is less serious. Frost got the basic story from a local history of Warren, New Hampshire, but his treatment of it fits into a tradition of folk humor in which the characters are eccentric, the comedy black, and moral judgment is suspended. The monologue is spoken by an old woman who is thought to be a witch—and a regular old harridan she is, too. Declared a pauper, she is a charge of the town of Wentworth, which has presented records in court to have her declared a citizen of Warren. There is dubious flattery, certainly, in having "two towns fighting / To make a present of me to each other." Not that it matters much to her where she lives, but the court records are wrong, and she proposes to be a thorough bitch of a witch by telling them so. Her shrewd motivation is petulantly declared:

> Right's right, and the temptation to do right
> When I can hurt someone by doing it
> Has always been too much for me, it has.

Part of the trouble is that she has not given enough "signs" that she really is a witch; as such, she might be a modest tourist attraction. The poem gradually becomes more personal, offering proof of her witchcraft for anyone with eyes to see it and giving an account of her marriage and her husband's unfortunate demise.

The story that she tells as proof of witchcraft also comes straight from the tradition of folk comedy; it is a tall tale that relies for its humor on the absurdity of its logic. She begins with an indignant rhetorical question:

It wa'n't no sign, I s'pose, when Mallice Huse
Said that I took him out in his old age
And rode all over everything on him
Until I'd had him worn to skin and bones,
And if I'd left him hitched unblanketed
In front of one Town Hall, I'd left him hitched
In front of every one in Grafton County.

Such a "sign" should have convinced most people, though it does seem rather secondhand, depending solely on the word of old Mr. Huse. But some "smarty someone," out of sheer perversity, set out to discredit the claim. He advised Mr. Huse to gnaw the posts he was allegedly hitched to, so that everyone could recognize his "trademark." Not a mark appeared on any of them. Instead, teeth marks were found on Mr. Huse's bedposts. "What did that prove?" asks the old woman, and we might well echo the sentiment. "But everybody took it for a proof," and that was that; she lost her claim to witchcraft.

Soon afterward she married Arthur Amy, the "smarty someone" who had begun his courting in such an unconventional manner. After the marriage he must have decided she had more value to him as a witch after all, and he tried to reestablish her claim to witchcraft. The manipulation of "the sound of sense" is doubly subtle at this point. All through the poem the witch has juggled past and present tenses with fine comic effect. Now she blends the intonations of Arthur Amy into her own monologue. She describes how he would ostentatiously make reference to her night flying (. . . "No, she ain't come back from kiting yet. / Last night was one of her nights out . . ."), or adopt a studied tone of resignation:

If anyone had seen me coming home
Over the ridgepole, 'stride of a broomstick,
As often as he had in the tail of the night,
He guessed they'd know what he had to put up with.

It all got too much for her, and Arthur Amy went the way of most husbands of witches:

I made him gather me wet snowberries
On slippery rocks beside a waterfall.
I made him do it for me in the dark.
And he liked everything I made him do.

It is the blandness of the statement here, the perverse logic of the woman's voice, that prevents us from taking it seriously or from passing moral judgment on her life. She has none of the self-consciousness of the woman in "A Servant to Servants," and her actions do not belong to the normal world of cause-and-effect. The other "characters" in the monologue—Mallice Huse and Arthur Amy—are one dimensional and comic. The comic effect is supported by the use of colloquial idioms ("It wa'n't no sign, I s'pose," "All is, if I'd a-known when I was young"); they give an eccentricity to the character. The beautifully controlled variations in her voice—righteous, petulant, cunning, indignant, bland—do not suggest variations in her character. That remains fixed, and because of this, she has none of the vulnerability that might make her tragic. The dramatic effect of the monologue remains essentially farcical, its comedy arising from a clash between an absurd illogicality of incident and the relentless logicality of the speaking voice.

Finally, there are those dramatic narratives that are more like regular dramas, involving the in-

teraction of two or more voices. Most of Frost's
dramatic poems fall into this category; they contain
all the elements of a stage play except length. "The
Fear" for instance, could easily be acted as a play
(more than four-fifths of its lines are dialogue and
the rest are stage directions), but a play of seventy
lines, lasting less than four minutes, would seem
slightly absurd. Indeed, it might suggest a slightness
in the theme, which is certainly not true of the written poem as Frost presents it. Not every dramatic
imagination finds its most suitable expression on the
stage—Henry James, for instance, failed dismally as
a playwright—and it would be a mistake to think of
Frost's dramatic narratives as being merely "failed
plays." What he did was to extend poetry as far as it
would go in the direction of pure drama while re-
taining the unity and succinctness of a poetic impression.

"The Fear" (1913) focuses on a single episode
that Frost witnessed one night when he was out
walking with his son—an episode in which a woman's most secret fear was brought to light. The
"action" is in the present and indeed seems slight
enough, but the ramifications of it go back into the
past. Some time before the present drama, the name-
less woman had left her husband and gone to live
with a man called Joel in a lonely farmhouse on a
remote country road. One dark night, driving home
with her lover, she sees a face in the bushes beside
the road. The image—so quickly glimpsed by the
light on the dashboard of the horse-drawn gig—acts
as a catalyst on her secret fear; the very certainty
of her assumptions, on such slight evidence, testifies
to the reality of her guilt and continual presence of

her fear. Why would anyone be lurking around her house so late at night? Or on such a lonely road? She leaps to the conclusion that it can only be her husband, come to claim vengeance, or "someone else he's sent to watch." When the horse and gig are in the barn, she voices her fears, and, acting against Joel's rationalizings, she takes the lantern out into the yard and challenges the darkness. Her question is not "Who's there?" but the more certain and apprehensive "What do you want?" After a pause a reply comes from along the road: "Nothing." And a passing stranger, holding a child by the hand, steps forward into the light to identify himself. They were simply out walking, he explains, because "Every child should have the memory / Of at least one long-after-bedtime walk." The ending might seem anticlimactic were it not for the fact that the center of the drama is the woman's mind; in terms of her fears it does not matter much who the man is or what he was doing. Whether from the tension, or the relief, or the realization that such an overt testimony of her feelings of guilt must inevitably change her relationship with Joel, she faints. The lantern clatters to the ground and goes out.

Frost's mode of narration exploits all the dramatic possibilities of the scene. The poem begins, as a play usually does, with a glimpse of the setting, after the couple have returned home; the dialogue does not begin until the eighth line. The setting is suitably gloomy and fear-ridden for the story:

> A lantern-light from deeper in the barn
> Shone on a man and woman in the door
> And threw their lurching shadows on a house
> Nearby, all dark in every glossy window.

Visually, the whole drama is a Gothic composition of darkness and pools of light and "lurching shadows." The only "stage property" throughout the poem is the lantern, and it is the focus for much of the action. It had been on the dashboard when they passed the face in the bushes. After they reach the barn and the woman decides to establish the truth of her fear, she asks Joel to hand it to her. He refuses on the logical ground that if there is a threat, the lantern light will only make her more vulnerable. She "pushed past him and got it for herself." As she stands in the middle of the yard, she holds the lamp in front of her skirt, looking over it into the night, until the "smell of scorching woolen made her faint." The last lines of the poem, like the first, focus on the lantern.

> The swinging lantern lengthened to the ground,
> It touched, it struck, it clattered and went out.

Obviously its visual role in the drama is important, but, inasmuch as it is the focus of two psychological attitudes, it has a thematic role too. For Joel, rational, and free from any feelings of fear because he cannot believe her husband would "care enough" to follow them, the lantern is seen in practical terms: if in danger, don't stand in a pool of light. For the woman, its value is psychological: the light is a kind of confessional in which she courageously challenges her subconscious fears to appear and be exorcised. Indeed, for her the symbolic value of the light has so far taken over the practical value, that she does not even notice how it scorches her skirt.

If the woman's psychological tension is the cen-

tral issue of the poem, this is highlighted by another
dramatic technique—the juxtaposing it with other
mental attitudes. Joel's calm logic acts as a foil to
her wild assumptions, and the rhythm of the blank
verse catches this contrast. Compare, for example,
the frantic effect of the woman's voice:

> Listen! He kicked a stone. Hear that, hear that!
> He's coming towards us. Joel, *go* in—please

with the soothing rationalization of Joel's:

> And if to see was what he wanted, why,
> He has seen all there was to see and gone.

The difference in effect is not simply a question
of rhythm (though it is no accident that the man's is
as regular as normal conversation and the woman's
keeps changing distractedly) but of the "sound of
sense," the voice posture that is so unmistakably
suggested by the dramatic context. Indeed, the poem
illustrates well what Frost meant when he praised
Edwin Arlington Robinson's play because "the action
is in the speech where it should be, and not along
beside it in antics for the body to perform." "The
Fear" contains barely sixteen lines of stage directions, and none of these are descriptive, telling us
how the voices are to sound. The voices speak for
themselves, and the stage directions are simply statements, such as "She pushed past him and got it for
herself."

The dramatic juxtaposition of the two voices,
however, does more than highlight the woman's
guilty fear. Subtly, it suggests a disunity in their relationship. Joel rationalizes clumsily, with the one
argument that a woman cannot bear to hear: "But

it's nonsense to think he'd care enough." At this, she is momentarily distracted from her present fear and answers him directly: "You mean you couldn't understand his caring." Nothing further is made of it, and it is curious to speculate on why Frost added this note. It goes beyond a question of vanity. "Caring" is at the heart of every human relationship, and almost all of the psychologically distraught characters of Frost's poems make some reference to it. It is more understated than "love," but, because it suggests responsibility, perhaps more important. The suggestion of a lack of "care" in this relationship removes the whole reason for existence for the woman, who, in abandoning her marriage, had staked everything on her present love. Almost subliminally, we are given an impression of an emotional emptiness that lies beyond her present fear, and perhaps partly explains it. In the light of this, the final juxtaposition of the obviously "caring" relationship of a father and son walking hand in hand in the night gives added poignancy.

In "The Fear" the focus is surely on the woman's mind, and the juxtaposition of other voices is simply used to highlight that. In "Home Burial" (1914), the drama lies in the conflict of two minds, a man's and a woman's. There is almost no action; the conflict is psychological. We see the husband and wife of this dramatic narrative at a moment of estrangement following the death of their baby son. The wife is utterly distraught—not so much, we suspect, at the death itself (though she indulges in that grief almost to the point of masochism) but at the attitude of her husband who seems so insensitive to it ("You *couldn't* care!"). His attitude is the more realistic, perhaps more masculine, one: life goes on. So, we learn in retrospect, he could dig the child's grave with his own hands, in the little family grave-yard near the house, leave his spade standing in the kitchen entry, and talk of everyday matters ("Three foggy mornings and one rainy day / Will rot the best birch fence a man can build"). By the time at which the poem is set—days, weeks, or perhaps months later—he has put the whole thing out of his mind to such an extent that it takes him a long while to realize that his wife always pauses at the top of the stairs because from the little window there she can see the grave.

Frost does not take sides in the presentation of these two attitudes; they are an aspect of the polar-ization and tension that he sees throughout the whole human and natural world and that he often drama-tizes through two separate voices. Often the two opposing voices are those of a man and woman, sometimes creative, sometimes destructive in their opposition. At their best, they are complementary rather than opposing principles. The young couple in "West-Running Brook," for instance, can trust them-selves to "go by contraries." But in "Home Burial" the masculine and the feminine attitudes are not held in any kind of delicate equipoise. There is really no resolution either—except that the wife's articulation of her resentment may be therapeutic, marking the beginning of a "cure." At least the husband seems to think so; but then he has never been particularly perceptive about her reactions. At the end of the poem she leaves the house despite his complacent assertion that "you have said it all and you feel bet-ter. / You won't go now."

"Home Burial" thus dramatizes the destructive result when complementary psychological attitudes become perverted and introspective. The man has indeed been insensitive to his wife's grief and singularly slow in divining the cause and extent of her resentment. Yet she is self-pitying and ungenerous not to recognize that grief has many expressions, and that a grim concentration on daily routine can be one of them.

Once more, the dramatic touches in the poem are sure and economical. The setting is the interior of the house, so claustrophobic that the woman feels she has to get out for air. The house is lonely, ancestral, belonging to *his* family. From the top of the stairs the window looks out to a family graveyard "not so much larger than a bedroom"—an apt detail that not only links the bed and the grave as parts of a natural process but touches on the cause of this marital estrangement. The only "action" in the drama is that the couple exchange places. At the beginning he is at the bottom of the stairs looking up at her; at the end he has climbed the stairs and she has come down and gone out the door. The reversal of position, without any real meeting, only emphasizes their separation. The essential conflict is contained in the dialogue and the distinctive voice posture of each. His voice is reasonable, pleading, courteous, bewildered: "And it's come to this, / A man can't speak of his own child that's dead." Hers is sulking, resentful, anguished:

> If you had any feelings, you that dug
> With your own hand—how could you?—his little
>   grave;
> I saw you from that very window there,

> Making the gravel leap and leap in air,
> Leap up, like that, like that, and land so lightly.

Finally, as in "The Fear," this intense psychological drama is given perspective by a glimpse of a larger, more normal, world. In "The Fear" the calm presence of a father and son out for a stroll gives us a measure of the woman's frantic state of mind. At the end of "Home Burial" we are told that "There's someone coming down the road!" and this detail highlights the intensely private nature of this quarrel. It is a grief so personal that appearances must be kept up, to protect it from outsiders.

Frost claimed that he drew the material for this poem from the situation of his wife's sister and her husband, who became estranged after the death of their first-born child in 1895; but the reaction of Elinor to the death of their own first-born in 1900 could not have been far from his mind. The same frustrations of blocked communication and destructive introspection dogged Frost's own marriage. In all his years of public readings, he never read this poem, perhaps because it was too personal.

In his dramatic narratives, Frost made his most distinctive contribution to poetry, and in the poetically sterile world of 1914, when many of them were published, he stood out with as much individuality as T. S. Eliot was to do a decade later. He created a new blank verse rhythm, wedded firmly to "the sound of sense" and capturing with accuracy and flexibility the sounds of the speaking voice. He gave poetry a new dimension, taking it as close to drama as it could possibly go. And in that Browningesque mold he created a range of characters and moods, a depth of psychological insight, and a technical mastery that no other poet has equaled. Not even Browning.

4

◆◆◆◆◆◆◆◆◆◆◆◆◆◆◆◆◆◆◆◆◆◆◆◆◆◆◆◆◆◆◆◆◆◆◆◆◆◆◆

Frost and the Sonnet Form

[A poem] begins in delight and ends in wisdom.
The figure is the same as for love.
    —preface to "The Figure a Poem Makes"

In a letter that Frost wrote to the American critic Lewis Chase in 1917, he listed some of his favorite poets and concluded the list with the comment: "But before all write me as one who cares most for the Shakespearean and Wordsworthian sonnets."[1] His own poetry reflects this preference. Frost probably wrote more first-rate sonnets than any other poet of this century; "Mowing," "Design," "Once by the Pacific," "The Oven Bird," "Range-Finding," "Putting in the Seed," "Acquainted with the Night," "Meeting and Passing," and "The Silken Tent," are among them. More succinctly than his other lyrics, Frost's sonnets illustrate his abiding concern for questions of form and metaphor.

His partiality for such a disciplined form at a time when poetry was moving away from conscious structure is a complex matter. It is related not only to his classical taste but, in a deeper way, to his psychological need for inner discipline as a way of coping with the chaotic forces of life itself. The insanity of his sister, the emotional instability of his daughter Irma, the depressions that led to his son's suicide and that made Frost himself "scared" of his own "desert places"—these were all tragic personal evidence of what could follow from the loss of an inner structure.

Thus, when Frost speaks of "form," the word has two levels of reference. On one level, it refers to all those elements of traditional prosody—rhyme, rhythm, meter, stanza pattern—with which he never ceased to be preoccupied. Indeed, the common sense of his technical statements about poetry—his ideas, for example, on the "sound of sense," on rhyming, on dramatic context, on the straining of rhythm and meter—tell us more about the real nature of the artistic process than more pretentious concepts such as Eliot's "objective correlative" or F. R. Leavis's "felt experience." Such prosodic concerns were, for Frost, the essence of writing poetry. Free verse, he claimed, was like "playing tennis with the net down." And each of these technical concerns was called into highly conscious play by the sonnet form.

But on a deeper, more philosophical level, Frost saw "form" as the cohering mental process behind all these technical elements. It is the catalyst by which chaos ("the vast chaos of all I have lived through") becomes meaning. As he wrote to the Amherst student newspaper in 1935:

We people are thrust forward out of the suggestions of form in the rolling clouds of nature. In us nature reaches its height of form and through us exceeds itself. When in doubt there is always form for us to go on with. Anyone who has achieved the least form to be sure of it, is lost to the larger excruciations. I think it must stroke faith the right way. . . .

The background is hugeness and confusion shading away from where we stand into black and utter chaos; and against the background any small man-made figure of order and concentration.[2]

Frost thus gives "form" the widest possible definition. It is the principle of order in the whole physical universe, by means of which the potential dissipation of the "rolling clouds of nature" is averted and channeled into the creation of man, a being with an intelligence capable, in turn, of controlling nature. In the "chaotic" welter of impressions and emotions in any individual life, it is only "form" that can shape such chaos into a direction and a meaning. In a poem, it is "form" alone that transmutes the vague intuition (the "lump in the throat") in which any poem has its origin into something that is understandable and communicable (a "clarification of life"). What all these aspects of form have in common is a tough-minded discipline. Not surprisingly, Frost was fond of making a parallel between athletic prowess and the writing of poetry: both are "performances," gaining their victories through stern rigor.

Close to this concept of form is Frost's concept of metaphor, to which he also gave the widest possible definition. Every creative thought rests on metaphor, he claimed, because every important thought is a "feat of association," "saying one thing in terms of another."

Metaphor is the intellectual principle by which the "tantalizing vagueness" of any creative intuition —be it scientific or artistic—finds its thought and takes communicable shape. To illustrate the point, Frost himself used metaphors to define what he meant by the term. Metaphor, he claimed, is a "prism" that takes raw "enthusiasm" and spreads it on a "screen," so that what had been simply a matter of feeling thus becomes a matter of perception.[3] Or, in a more homely analogy, it is a napkin ring: "Like a napkin, we fold the thought, squeeze it through the ring, and it expands once more."[4] What is common to both these metaphoric definitions is a sense of strain or tension. All meaningful thought is hard won, demanding both discipline and detachment. "The only materialist," wrote Frost, ". . . is the man who gets lost in his material without a gathering metaphor to throw it into shape and order. He is the lost soul."[5]

Form, then, creates meaning. And, in a very real

sense, it is the meaning. Nothing demonstrates this more clearly than the concentrated form of the sonnet. Like Coleridge and Emerson, Frost believed that a poem was essentially organic. It creates itself, having been given direction from "the first line laid down"; or, as Frost expressed it in a memorable image: "Like a piece of ice on a hot stove, the poem must ride on its own melting." If a poem is simply written to a formula, or if it is written to build up to a previously chosen final line—if the "clarification," in other words, occurs before the poem has begun—then the rationale, the creative impetus, of the poem is gone, and the poem will be bad, dishonest.

[The poet's] intention is of course a particular mood that won't be satisfied with anything less than its own fulfillment. . . . One thing to know it by: it shrinks shyly from anticipatory expression. Tell love beforehand and, as Blake says, it loses flow without filling the mould; the cast will be a reject. The freshness of a poem belongs absolutely to its not having been thought out and then set to verse. . . . A poem is the emotion of having a thought while the reader waits a little anxiously for the success of dawn. The only discipline to begin with is the inner mood that at worst may give the poet a false start or two like the almost microscopic filament of cotton that goes before the blunt thread-end and must be picked up first by the eye of the needle.[6]

To a certain extent, any poet who is struggling to fulfill such an inner mood will have his expression determined, perhaps even limited, by the techniques that belong to his craft. Like the painter or the musician, the poet has only a certain number of tools available to him. If he is writing in English, Frost would say, he has basically a choice of two meters (Frost refused to acknowledge more than "strict iambic" and "loose iambic"); he has a choice of "any length of line up to six feet"; and he can use "an assortment of line lengths for any shape of stanza." Not much with which to do battle with chaos or to fulfill an inner mood that is crying for articulation. But more than adequate if the poet has enough faith to put himself in league with his own tools. Frost illustrated this creative determinism of form beautifully with reference to one of Shakespeare's sonnets:

Suppose him to have written down "When in disgrace with Fortune and men's eyes." He has uttered about as much as he has to live up to in the theme as in the form. Odd how the two advance into the open pari passu. He has given out that he will descend into Hades, but he has confided in no one how far before he will turn back, or whether he will turn back at all, and by what jutting points of rock he will pick his way. He may proceed as in blank verse. Two lines more, however, and he has let himself in for rhyme, three more and he has set himself a stanza. Up to this point his discipline has been the self-discipline whereof it is written in so great praise. The harsher discipline from without is now well begun. He who knows not both knows neither. His wordly commitments are now three or four deep. Between us, he was no doubt bent on the sonnet in the first place from habit, and what's the use in pretending he was a freer agent than he had any ambition to be? He had made most of his commitments all in one plunge. The only suspense he asks us to share with him is in the theme. He goes down, for instance, to a depth that must surprise him as much as it does us. But he doesn't even have the say of how long his piece will be. Any worry is as to whether he will outlast or last out the fourteen lines—have to cramp or stretch to come out even—have enough bread for the butter or butter for the bread. As a matter of fact, he gets through in twelve lines and doesn't know quite what to do with the last two.[7]

If we needed proof, then, that Frost was a poet with a classic sense of form, it would surely lie in his fondness for what is perhaps the most consciously structured verse form in English. Yet, never a slave to convention, he experimented to a highly original degree with the rhythm, rhyme, structure, and even theme of the traditional sonnet. The success of his experimentation may be ascertained most clearly if we examine three of his sonnets, separated in date, and all differing in theme and tone: "Putting in the Seed" (1914), "Design" (1922), and "The Silken Tent" (1939).

PUTTING IN THE SEED

You come to fetch me from my work tonight
When supper's on the table, and we'll see
If I can leave off burying the white
Soft petals fallen from the apple tree
(Soft petals, yes, but not so barren quite,
Mingled with these, smooth bean and wrinkled pea),
And go along with you ere you lose sight
Of what you came for and become like me,
Slave to a springtime passion for the earth.
How Love burns through the Putting in the Seed
On through the watching for that early birth
When, just as the soil tarnishes with weed,
The sturdy seedling with arched body comes
Shouldering its way and shedding the earth crumbs.

The rigorous sonnet form is used here to encompass a series of oppositions (birth and burial, "white" and "tarnished," "smooth" and "wrinkled," "you" and "I") and to unite them all in the central symbol of the "seed." The very tautness of the form controls the dramatic change from the colloquial voice of the first sentence ("You come to fetch me . . . and we'll see") to the more solemn statement in the second ("How Love burns . . ."), just as it controls the parallel development from the simple realistic act of burying the apple petals to the strong sexuality of the later imagery.

The sonnet is basically Shakespearean in form, though the rhyme scheme is narrower than that of Shakespeare, working as it does with only five rhymes (abab, abab, cdcd, ee) instead of Shakespeare's usual seven. Nor is the final couplet a summarizing epigram like that of Shakespeare; in fact, the structure, with its single break occurring after the ninth line, is more Miltonic. The conscious changes that Frost thus makes in the traditional sonnet form illustrate his theory of the organic growth of a poem. The emerging poem dictates its own variations.

"Putting in the Seed" falls into two sections, two sentences, though the break in the rhyme scheme is oddly out of phase with the syntactical break. The first nine-line section lays down the elements of what is later to be enlarged through metaphor to a more universal comment. The scene is homely: a man is working on a spring evening, burying the fallen petals from his apple tree while he waits for his wife's call to supper. His digging is practical, of course, but the work is really a labor of love. His voice is equally homely (apart from the jarring awkwardness of the parentheses in lines 5–6), taking on an easy colloquialness through the slight irregularity of the iambic meter. The whole scene is simply a country tableau until we come against the ninth line: "Slave to a springtime passion for the earth." This line is given special focus by the fact that syntactically it belongs to the octet, yet the rhyme pushes it into the sestet.

It is as if this central line were being pulled in two directions at once, making it the pivot on which the meaning of the poem turns.

The vocabulary is here modulated to prepare for the enlargement of theme in the second section. "Slave . . . to passion" gives a human dimension to all the evidence of spring fecundity in the fallen apple blossoms. As such, it links the delicate suggestions of shared love and insight throughout the first section ("You come . . . and we'll see / If I can leave off . . . And go along with you ere you . . . become like me") with the stronger images of sexual love in the second. From the broader standpoint of this ninth line, we can look back and note the unexplored paradox in some of the realistic details so far: the "burying" of "white" petals is part of this "passion"; the soft petals are "not so barren quite," containing within them the seeds of renewal.

In the five-line second section all these metaphorical implications are brought into the open. The capitalization of "Love" and "Putting in the Seed" fixes the theme of human sexuality clearly, as do words like "burns," "birth," and "arched body." Yet how exactly human generation is seen to parallel natural generation! The "putting in the seed," whether human or plant, leads miraculously to fruition, to the sturdy seedling "shouldering" its way to the air as instinctively as a child does in birth. The sheer inexorableness of the process from seedtime to fruition is strongly captured. And the very interrelatedness of the two images of birth—that of the plant bursting through the ground, "shedding the earth crumbs" and that of the human "seedling" with "arched body" "shouldering" its way into the world—gives both tact

and strength to the whole poem. Yet within the physical exactness of the imagery such details as "soil
tarnished with weeds" and "shedding the earth
crumbs" carry a metaphorical weight that goes beyond simple physicality. There is at once a sense of
all the limitations of a "tarnished" post-Edenic world,
and an intimation of the spirit's triumph over its
physical embodiment as it shoulders its way "shedding
the earth crumbs."

"Putting in the Seed" is a beautifully constructed
sonnet. Its central metaphor moves easily from the
particular to the universal in the smooth shift from
one sentence to the second. Yet its ultimate value
rests primarily in the aptness of the metaphorical
parallel between natural and human generation, the
exactness of its observations, and the tact that controls it. There is no intellectual resolution of the
parallel. We are left only with a sense of wonder:
"How Love burns. . . ."

A later sonnet, "Design," has far more intellectual
tautness.

DESIGN

I found a dimpled spider, fat and white,
On a white heal-all, holding up a moth
Like a white piece of rigid satin cloth—
Assorted characters of death and blight
Mixed ready to begin the morning right,
Like the ingredients of a witches' broth—
A snow-drop spider, a flower like a froth,
And dead wings carried like a paper kite.

What had that flower to do with being white,
The wayside blue and innocent heal-all?
What brought the kindred spider to that height,
Then steered the white moth thither in the night?

What but design of darkness to appall?—
If design govern in a thing so small.

Here the metaphor is carried much further than a simple parallel and an expression of wonder at it. The central image of the "design," in its conjunction of the spider, the flower (a white heal-all), and the moth, is far more complex, more fraught with intrinsic paradox, than the "seed" of the earlier sonnet. And Frost carries it further. It becomes the focus for a subtle questioning of one of the traditional arguments for the existence of God—the argument that, just as a clock implies a clockmaker, so the the evident design in the physical world implies a Designer. This reasoning is commonly known as the "argument from design."

The basic structure of "Design" is Petrarchan; the situation is presented in the octet and resolved, after a definite break, in the sestet. But the structure also follows the traditional sequence of logical debate: first the presentation of the facts, then the questioning of them, then the resolution. The scheme, revolving around only four rhymes, is even tighter and more concentrated than in most Petrarchan sonnets. It is as if the terrifying implications of meaninglessness that the poem hints at demanded a highly disciplined form to bring them within the domain of human comprehension. The greater the threat of dissipation in the subject, the tighter the conscious form needed to hold it in. "Design" has an aptness of form that is absolutely faultless.

The octet presents, without any authorial comment, a simple nature scene: a spider and a moth on a white flower in the morning freshness. Deliberately, it builds up the impression of normality; the whole

impact of the sestet would be lost if we simply accepted this scene as an aberration. If the poem is to
be a wicked reversal of the argument from design,
then it must challenge that argument by its own
logic. It therefore concedes the immediate point. An
apparent design in all things implies an original Designer. Granted. But if the apparent design is one of
horror, what kind of Designer? What immortal hand
or eye dare frame the awful symmetry of this scene?
The necessary impression of normality is created
partly by the beautiful regularity of the form, partly
by the cheery colloquialness of the speaker's tone
("mixed ready to begin the morning right"), but
mostly by the careful choice of words that are usually
associated with innocence and freshness ("dimpled,"
"white," "snow-drop," "froth," "satin").

Yet, undercutting this careful normality the effect is one of horror, just as the most chilling mani-
festation of insanity is the one that is camouflaged by
an apparent rationality. Each element that helps to
create the surface normality here is paradoxically,
chillingly, negated by the context of the total "mix-
ture." The regularity of form, for example, is mocked
by the visual symmetry of this study in white. The
colloquial tone creates a reassurance that is denied by
the "appalling" scene that gradually unfolds. Finally,
the innocuous words, when linked to this context, become horrifyingly perverted.

The first line rollicks along in perfectly regular
iambics. "Dimpled" modifies any shock in finding the
word "spider," and "fat" modifies it further. This is
the kind of spider that Miss Muffet might have en-
countered. "White," given emphasis by ending the
line, pulls us up. A white spider? Even if Poe and

Melville had not previously attuned us to the ambiguities of whiteness, the disquieting contradiction here sounds the first jarring note. It rings again in the second line. The "heal-all" (so-called because of certain healing properties assigned to it) is a little blue flower found all over New England ("The wayside blue and innocent heal-all"). Here its very name contributes to the mockery of the poem, and its unusual albino form seems ominously unnatural, like that of the spider. The final ingredient in the scene is a moth, also "white," but white and "rigid" with the "satin" patina of death, and completely denaturalized, simply "like a . . . piece of . . . cloth."

The resonance of the words throughout the octet is extraordinary; the poem begins to reverberate on many levels of association. Note, for example, how the ritual action of the spider's "holding up" the moth makes him seem like the celebrant of a mass—not a black mass, despite the diabolism of the scene, but a perversely white one. The resonance continues in the three-line parenthesis (lines 4–6). "Assorted characters" suggests a group of strolling players acting out a ritual dance of death. They are "assorted," implying their separate identities, yet "mixed," implying a conscious (and diabolical) Mixer, the first thrust at the argument from design. "Mixed ready to begin the morning right." Even the obvious pun on "rite" cannot destroy the terrible heartiness here—like the terrible heartiness of Macbeth's witches presaging "so foul and fair a day." The summary of the scene in the last two lines of the octet refocuses and intensifies each ingredient. The spider is now "a snow-drop spider," its identity blurring into that of a flower. "A flower like a froth" sounds delicate and fluffy, except that "froth," partly because of the rhyme, has associations with the ominous "broth" of the witches. And the solemn spondees of "dead wings carried" sound a dirge for the victim of the little drama, now as transparent and skeletal as a "paper kite."

The facts having thus been marshaled, the "argument" proceeds with strict philosophical method in the sestet. The first question ("What had that flower to do with being white?") goes beyond ontology to question the whole notion of guilt or responsibility in a seemingly arbitrary world. The second ("What brought the kindred spider to that height, / Then steered the white moth thither in the night?") is more malicious; the word "steered" hints at a conscious Malevolence behind it all. The questions are resolved by a rhetorical question: "What but design of darkness to appall?" All the images of horrifying whiteness become fused in a "design of darkness." The concept of a Manichean universe, of a world created by the forces of darkness, is the only logical conclusion of this perverse argument from design.

But the poem does not end with the thirteenth line. The final line is a poetic tour de force, the whole poem moving relentlessly to its conclusion: "If design govern in a thing so small." "If" is the crucial word; it opens up two possible interpretations. Perhaps, it might be arguing, it is indeed foolish to use such a trivial scene as an argument for or against design; design does *not* govern in a thing so small. But if not there, where? The other possibility is terrifying—that there is no design at all in the world, not even a Manichean one. The whiteness simply mirrors an absurd blankness. The poem thus concludes with a philosophical checkmate.

"Design" is a poem of terror whichever way we look at it. And it achieves its impact by the very tautness of its expression. What the sonnet form did was to set the rigorous boundaries to that expression. The challenge then was to tighten the ideas so that, within those boundaries, every word carries weight. Just how much Frost tightened his ideas may be seen clearly by comparing our present version of "Design" with its original version entitled "In White."

> A dented spider like a snowdrop white
> On a white Heal-all, holding up a moth
> Like a white piece of lifeless satin cloth—
> Saw ever curious eye so strange a sight?
> Portent in little, assorted death and blight
> Like the ingredients of a witches' broth?
> The beady spider, the flower like a froth,
> And the moth carried like a paper kite.
>
> What had that flower to do with being white,
> The blue Brunella every child's delight?
> What brought the kindred spider to that height?
> (Make we no thesis of the miller's plight.)
> What but design of darkness and of night?
> Design, design! Do I use the word aright?[8]

How lame it all sounds! The central idea is there, though not the subtlety of the final twist. A few of the images are already in place—"snowdrop," "satin cloth," the "witches' broth," "froth," and "paper kite." But the most obvious similarity is the form—not simply the choice of the sonnet, but the octet-sestet structure and the sequential argument. If Frost had dropped the notion of a sonnet and had continued to refine his argument into another stanza, "In White" would probably never have progressed beyond the barely competent poem it is. Instead, given the limited number of lines and metrical feet in his chosen form, he concentrated on making each one of them count. Note, for example, how the substitution of "rigid" for "lifeless" in line 3 adds the suggestion of rigor mortis, or "dimpled" for "dented" in line 1 adds a babylike innocence that will later be dramatically undercut. "Brunella," as a name for the heal-all, and "miller" (a miller is a moth with powdery wings) are altogether too localized and coy. The change in line 13 from the pointlessly repetitive "design of darkness and of night" to "design of darkness to appall" is masterly; and Frost was too word conscious to have been unaware of the deadly pun of "pall" in "appall." But his critical faculties are proved most clearly in the complete scrapping of the worst three lines of the original poem—lines 4, 12, and 14, all of them loose, sententious, and banal. Their substitutes are firm and hard hitting, stretched taut by the sheer discipline of the form.

Finally, let us look at a sonnet that is totally different in tone from either "Putting in the Seed" or "Design": "The Silken Tent." We have to go back to the Elizabethans or the seventeenth-century poets to find anything like the tonal delicacy of this love poem.

> THE SILKEN TENT
> She is as in a field a silken tent
> At midday when a sunny summer breeze
> Has dried the dew and all its ropes relent,
> So that in guys it gently sways at ease,
> And its supporting central cedar pole,
> That is its pinnacle to heavenward
> And signifies the sureness of the soul,

Seems to owe naught to any single cord,
But strictly held by none, is loosely bound
By countless silken ties of love and thought
To everything on earth the compass round,
And only by one's going slightly taut
In the capriciousness of summer air
Is of the slightest bondage made aware.

The way the sonnet is built on the elaboration of
a single metaphor, the studied obliqueness of its emotional impulse, the controlled complexity of its one-
sentence syntax, and the subtle modulations of its
phrasing—all recall an Elizabethan sense of formal
beauty, while the "mechanical" image of the tent pole
seems as unromantically apposite—as "metaphysical"
in the technical sense—as Donne's unromantic image
of the compass. The rhyme scheme and, in a less
strict way, the structure are also Elizabethan. The
structure seems to have no break after quatrain or
octet, though in fact there are very definite progres-
sions. The image of the tent in the first four lines
shifts to the image of the tent pole in the second four.
By the time we get to lines 9–11, the analogy with the
woman—established in the first words of the sonnet
("She is as . . .") and then held in suspension—begins
to take over, and the emphasis is on the positive quality of her apparent independence. In the final three
lines there is a gentle reminder that the bondage,
though loose, does exist, and that it is always suscepti-
ble to the "capriciousness" of life's pulls.

The metaphor is subtly enlarged throughout the
poem. As in "Putting in the Seed" its strength as a
metaphor lies in the exactness of observation that
sustains both levels of the analogy. On the realistic
level the image is a scrupulously exact one. The tent

is held upright both by a central tent pole which supports the actual cloth, and by several guy ropes attached to the cloth, which radiate out in several directions and are pegged to the ground. The ropes act as a support for the central pole and prevent it from falling in any one direction. The phenomenon described in lines 2–3 is also a realistically exact one. When the ropes are wet with rain or dew they contract and the strain on the pole is increased, making it firmly fixed. When they dry out in the sunlight this strain relents; the tent pole may sway a little, but not too far, since the encircling ropes will always maintain a basic equilibrium. The tent pole thus "seems" to be independent, but in fact is not; similarly the ropes "seem" to be binding, but in fact allow a certain freedom and flexibility. This is the basic paradox of the image that Frost develops into metaphor.

The enlargement of the image to a metaphorical level is begun in the very choice of words that establishes its realistic level. The word "relent," for instance. It is technically correct, but it also carries overtones of a merciful relief from strain, a sense that is repeated in "at ease." The metaphysical connotations become more obvious in the phrase "pinnacle to heavenward" and reach direct statement by the time we get to line 7, when the tent pole is seen to "signify the sureness of the soul." The metaphor is now working on its two levels. The woman's soul is seen as having that "independent dependence" that Frost so admired in people. It supports the whole "tent," which gives shading and protection to all. In its steadfastness it "seems" to be independent, to "owe naught to any single cord"; yet in fact it is given strength and support by the encircling guy ropes of "countless silken ties of love and thought."

The richness of the poem rests in the paradoxical attitude to the "ties." They give support and strength certainly; without them the "tent" would collapse. On the metaphorical level of the analogy, they are the human ties, the "promises to keep," that give the woman her lovely humanity. They are "loose," un-obsessive, but they are there. "Silken," and ranging "the compass round," they yet bind her. The idea of "bondage" is mentioned twice, though each time it is qualified by the mention of its "slightness." The end of the poem is linked to the beginning through this sense of bondage. In the first quatrain the idea of the ropes "relenting" and leaving the tent "at ease" implies that they were in a binding tension before the midday breeze dried them. The last three lines of the poem again emphasize that the freedom is only apparent, liable to be jerked back to a realization of its ties by any capricious fate.

Indeed, the notion of "realization," and the differ-ence between appearance and reality, are central to the poem. The woman "seems" to "owe naught to any single cord," yet she is "made aware" that such ap-pearances are deceptive. Both "seems" and "aware" are given added rhythmic emphasis by the position each holds in its respective line. She is free yet not free, "bound" but "loosely," reaching "to heaven-ward" yet anchored to the earth, "sure" in soul only because she is responsive to the ties that sustain her. In the economical precision of this paradoxical metaphor Frost captures more of the essentially ambivalent quality of love and spiritual strength than a dozen rhapsodic love poems eulogizing assorted parts of the anatomy.

The story is told of a student in a creative writ-ing class who claimed: "I've finished a short story.

Now I just have to go back over it and put in the symbols." Frost's poems are never like that. His "symbols" are integral, and his poems grow organically, expanding the metaphors logically, assuming direction "from the first line laid down." It was form that created a poem, and this is nowhere more evident than in the strict form of the sonnet. The discipline of form gave Frost his emotional distance from the subject, the distance that he called ulteriority. (He used to quip that he had an "ulteriority complex.") The best description of the way in which form works as a discovery or "clarification" of life, a human victory over the "crudity" of raw material, is given in his own words:

The most exciting movement in nature is not progress, advance, but expansion and contraction, the opening and shutting of the eye, the hand, the heart, the mind. We throw our arms wide with a gesture of religion to the universe; we close them around a person. We explore and adventure for a while and then we draw in to consolidate our gains. The breathless swing is between subject matter and form.[9]

5

The Meditative Voice
. . . Some Major Themes

They cannot scare me with their empty spaces
Between stars—on stars where no human race is.
I have it in me so much nearer home
To scare myself with my own desert places.
                              —*"Desert Places"*

It is one of the anomalies of Frost's reputation that he has, on the one hand, been enshrined by the American public as a kind of grass-roots philosopher, and, on the other hand, been attacked by various critics for his lack of any systematic philosophy, for being, as Yvor Winters called him, a "spiritual drifter" who lacked the intellectual toughness of a Yeats or an Eliot. Both attitudes are perhaps misguided in their concept of a poet and in their assessment of Frost. He *was* concerned with philosophical questions, though in a random way, and he carried certain preoccupations through many of his poems, expanding and refining the issues they raised. In this chapter some of these basic preoccupations will be examined through poems that are more intellectual or speculative than any looked at so far. Their basic impulse is meditative. In them the focus is not so much on character and action (as in the dramatic narratives) or on a particular emotion (as in the lyrics) as on the resolution of a problem. The interest in the speaking voice is still there, because the problem is usually formulated in terms of a human situation; but the emphasis is on the problem itself rather than on the speaker.

Certainly, Frost was not a systematic thinker. He was against systems on principle. "I'm afraid of too much structure," he once wrote. "Some violence is always done to the wisdom you build a philosophy out of."[1] Part of his suspiciousness toward "structure" lay in the fact that "wisdom" could so easily lose itself in questions of political or ideological debate, in "grievances" rather than "griefs." One needed to get beyond mere debate: "Get up there high enough and the differences that make controversy become only the two legs of a body the weight of which is on one in one period, on the other in the next. . . . I have wanted to find ways to transcend the strife-method."[2] But essentially he would have been suspicious of anything that implied a single answer. He was born too late to be reassured by Emerson's cheerful monism.

If the subjects of Frost's meditative poems tend to be disparate and inconclusive, simply "momentary stays against confusion," they at least deal with complex and important issues. Exploratory and speculative, they represent a lonely pondering on the central problems of existence: man's identity and freedom, his relation to the natural world and the flux of time, his defenses against an engulfing chaos, the place of human suffering and the possibility of salvation. His poems are torn, as his life was, between affirmation and negation, and if the resolution of this conflict seems at best tenuous, that tenuousness is deliberate. Essentially a pragmatist, Frost was less concerned with chronicling the spirit of his age, as Eliot was, or with forging his insights into a philosophical system, as Wallace Stevens was, than with working out a practical *modus vivendi*, a way of making something out of the facts that life presented him with.

One extremity of the philosophical spectrum that Frost's mind sought to encompass finds expression in the poems of terror that Lionel Trilling referred to. This is the pull of the annihilating dark, the fear of his "own desert places." The personal tragedies in his life added poignancy to the basic question of whether "all the soul-and-body scars / Were not too much to pay for birth." Intellectually he had even taken the step beyond the romantic awareness of personal despair to contemplate the possibility of cosmic meaninglessness. "Design" and "Neither Out Far Nor In Deep" give us a glimpse of absurd and absolute blankness, just as Melville's "Bartleby" does. But, unlike Melville, Frost never steps into this blankness to explore its bleak reality, and his poetry thus lacks that dimension of intellectual daring. He does not even create a positive metaphor for it. Perhaps Frost could not afford to risk his precarious sanity. Like his drumlin woodchuck, who at the first suggestion of an overwhelming "alarm" goes back to his "strategic retreat," Frost looked on chaos and refused to enter it.

Very few of Frost's poems are as unequivocally affirmative as "Bereft" or "Acquainted with the Night" are unequivocally negative. In most of them a sense of affirmation is hard won, with a realistic awareness of its opposite clearly present in the poem. It is rarely simplistic or moralistic; the threat of its negation is too close for that. In "The Onset," for example, the speaker's firm conviction in the second stanza ("I know that winter death has never tried / The earth but it has failed") is given dramatic balance by the fact that it grows out of the bleak subjective picture of winter desolation in the first half of the poem. In "Come In" we have seen how the jaunty resolution to stay outside the woods is balanced by the temptation to "come in." In "Our Hold on the Planet," the fact that the affirmation is a minimal one is emphasized by the rational, cautious voice of the speaker debating the "just proportion of good to ill" in the conflict between man and nature:

> Take nature altogether since time began,
> Including human nature, in peace and war,
> And it must be a little more in favor of man,
> Say a fraction of one percent at the very least.

A fraction of one percent. Hardly a Whitmanesque, or even an Emersonian, optimism. If Frost's poetry on the whole is positive in its attitude to life, the affirmation is scarcely exuberant.

Yet his overall attitude is positive, despite a temperamental bias toward negation, and it is won through a conscious and tough-minded pragmatism. Pragmatism is the general philosophical premise behind most of Frost's poetry and the specific concern of such poems as "Hyla Brook" and "Mowing." If his refusal to follow his intuitions of meaninglessness through to an intellectual conclusion denied his poetry the tragic intensity of Melville, this was partly due to a courageous awareness that life has to be lived on its own terms. Opting out, like Bartleby, is no answer. Hamlet, after all, with whom Frost sometimes identified himself, had debated whether it was "nobler in the mind" to go on living or to commit suicide. Frost saw his confrontation with existence in terms of the same moral and intellectual imperatives.

His attitude in this was reinforced by the contemporary philosopher and psychologist, William James, who taught at Harvard from 1872 to 1907. By one of those unfortunate quirks of chance, James was away on leave the year that Frost enrolled for philosophy there, but Frost studied his book *The Will to Believe* as a text in the course. Years later, he could assert: "My greatest inspiration, when I was a student, was a man whose classes I never attended."

James himself had contemplated suicide at the age of twenty-eight, so that the philosophical justifications that made him choose life and rise to such eminence in the intellectual world were particularly relevant to the young Robert Frost. Although he had not yet formalized his philosophy of pragmatism, James based his commitment to living on the practical grounds of creating one's own human meaning and value rather than on orthodox Christian attitudes to faith. "Belief" was important not because there was an

absolute deity who demanded or deserved it but because it was humanly necessary for the business of
living. Unlike Emerson, James was skeptical, doubting, yet determined to use his doubts in a positive
way. His "self-reliance" is far more tentative and
courageous than that of Emerson; it is what Frost
meant later by "falling forward in the dark."

In "Is Life Worth Living?", one of the essays in
The Will to Believe, James sums up the essence of
his belief:

So far as man stands for anything, and is productive or
originative at all, his entire vital function may be said to
have to deal with maybes. Not a victory is gained, not a
deed of faithfulness or courage is done, except upon a
maybe; not a service, not a sally of generosity, not a scientific exploration or experiment or textbook, that may not
be a mistake. It is only by risking our persons from one
hour to another that we live at all.[3]

The question of whether life is worth living can
only be handled subjectively; it is up to oneself:

If you surrender to the nightmare view and crown the evil
edifice by your own suicide, you have indeed made a picture totally black. Pessimism, completed by your act, is
true beyond a doubt, so far as your world goes. . . . But
suppose, on the other hand, that instead of giving way to
the nightmare view you cling to it that this world is not
the *ultimatum*. . . . Suppose, however thickly evils crowd
upon you, that your unconquerable subjectivity proves to
be their match, and that you find a more wonderful joy
than any passive pleasure can bring in trusting ever in the
larger whole. Have you not now made life worth living on
these terms? What sort of a thing would life really be with
your qualities ready for a tussle with it, if it only brought
fair weather and gave these higher faculties of yours no
scope?[4]

Life is thus both given and made; what we make of what we are given is the only important issue.

There were many things about James's philosophy that appealed to Frost. Frost was agnostic enough to need a philosophy that would justify itself in purely human terms and yet would satisfy the spiritual and intuitive in him; James's emphasis on self-realization did that. Perhaps more importantly, Frost was temperamentally receptive to the moral commitments that James demanded—the courage, will, effort, that were needed to choose life and to propel the "maybes" into positive action. All through Frost's writing we find such ideas reoccurring, the Jamesian vocabulary unchanged—words such as courage ("courage is the ability to go ahead on insufficient knowledge"), will ("every poem is . . . a figure of the will braving alien entanglements"), effort ("the effort, the essay of love"), hero ("it takes a hero to make a poem"); words such as "risk," "tussle," "threat." Frost might have reached a similar position independently —that James's ideas should have had the effect that they did indicates Frost's receptivity—but most of Frost's major themes carry the stamp of Jamesian philosophy.

The basic premise, then, is a conscious, pragmatic acceptance of life as it is. "I wouldn't give a cent to see the world . . . made better. . . . I have no quarrel with the material,"[5] Frost wrote to a young poet in 1930, and he held that view throughout his life. With a certain self-righteousness he poured scorn on T. S. Eliot and other prophets of doom who saw the 1920s as fragmented and sterile, the worst of all possible ages. In a letter to the Amherst student newspaper in 1935, he wrote:

. . . you will often hear it said that the age of the world we live in is particularly bad. I am impatient of such talk. We have no way of knowing that this age is one of the worst in the world's history. Arnold claimed the honor for the age before this. Wordsworth claimed it for the last but one. . . . I say they claimed the honor for their ages. They claimed it rather for themselves. It is immodest of a man to think of himself as going down before the worst forces ever mobilized by God. . . . Whatever progress may be taken to mean, it can't mean making the world any easier a place in which to save your soul—or if you dislike hearing your soul mentioned in open meeting, say your decency, your integrity.[6]

Frost repeated the ideas of this letter in his didactic poem "The Lesson for Today" (1941). But the theme of simple acceptance occurs as early as *A Boy's Will* (1913). In one of the poems of that volume, "Mowing," the speaker listens to his scythe "whispering" to the ground. Meditating on the question "What was it it whispered?" he summarily dismisses any idea that it is whispering about such fanciful things as "the gift of idle hours" or "easy gold at the hand of fay or elf." No, it is whispering, as far as he can guess, of practical, substantial things—the "heat of the sun" or the "lack of sound," for

> Anything more than the truth would have seemed too weak
> To the earnest love that laid the swale in rows.

There is not the usual attitude here toward fact and fancy. There is no sense of loss because a fancy is dismissed, no feeling that reality is a dull substitute. "The fact is the sweetest dream that labor knows," the speaker concludes. The fact. No realist could ask for more.

In Frost's pugnacious acceptance of such facts, there is little of the sense of wonder that has characterized much of American writing. He concludes "Hyla Brook," for instance, with the simple statement, "We love the things we love for what they are." They are not really very much, as the description in that poem of the dried-up summer brook, carrying only a memory of its spring force, implies. But we love the sheer "fact" of them.

As part of this tough, pragmatic acceptance of life as it is, Frost accepts the limitations of human knowledge and capacity. Commenting on the folly of bringing a peach tree too far north into New England for it to have a fair chance of survival, the speaker of "There Are Roughly Zones" recognizes that "There are roughly zones whose laws must be obeyed," though he has a sneaking admiration for "this limitless trait in the hearts of men" that will gamble on defying the "zones." Again, in "Too Anxious for Rivers," Frost picks up the theme of recognizing that there are "roughly zones" beyond which the human imagination should not trespass. "No place to get lost like too far in the distance," the prudent speaker of that poem notes. Man can get lost in the metaphysical "distance" just as easily as he can face annihilation in the dark "woods." Pragmatically, cannily, Frost thus plots the battleground of his own endeavor; his "zone" is realistic, practical, circumscribed by an awareness of its human limitations. Perhaps his most apt metaphor for such endeavor is that of the "swinger of birches," who likes his aspirations "toward heaven" to land him squarely back on earth again.

Such a recognition of human limitations may seem an unfashionable virtue to our post-Renaissance

sensibility, and it is easy to misinterpret Frost's acceptance of reality as easy passivity. In fact his acceptance
is rarely easy and never passive. To think of him as a
"spiritual drifter" is to miss the point. It is to ignore
not only the tough practicality behind the affirmations
of his poetry, but also the intellectual justification he
sought to give them. In poem after poem Frost strove
to establish some intellectual basis for his hard-won
emotional affirmation.

"The Trial by Existence" (1913) is one such attempt. It is not a good poem. The phrasing is stilted,
the imagery is immemorable and not organically related to the theme, there is an occasional lapse into
"poetic diction," and the exposition of ideas is cloudy.
Only the theme—clumsy and didactic though it is—is
worth looking at twice. The poem is set in a state of
preexistence, similar to that in Blake's *Book of Thel,*
and it hinges on two main ideas. One is that the
souls about to be born actually choose an earthly
existence, and choose it foreknowing both its joys and
sorrows. The human soul, when it is born, is thus
"heroic," "valiant," and, above all, free. But there is a
catch. Life would be too easy and conducive to pride
if, at any moment of "agony or strife," the soul could
comfort itself with the realization that it had freely
chosen such an act of "daring." The second idea,
therefore, is that at birth, God obliterates the "lasting
memory . . . / That life has for us on the wrack /
Nothing but what we somehow chose." The human
soul is still heroic, but it does not know that it is. It
has to prove its daring all over again, to justify itself
in a "trial by existence."

The poem thus presents a Jamesian answer to
the Jamesian question "Is Life Worth Living?" though

Frost began his poem as early as 1892, before he had read James. Heroic will, conscious choice, self-definition through suffering: these are the concepts through which Frost tried to find an intellectual rationale for his pragmatism, his acceptance of life as it is. At a time when naturalism, with its philosophy of pessimistic determinism, had a strong foothold in American literature, Frost refused to admit that men's fate might be determined by such factors as heredity or environment. His concepts of individualism and self-reliance were as strong as Emerson's, though more existential, more grounded in the idea that man not only improves himself but actually creates himself, defines himself, through taking on a "trial."

These ideas of will, choice, and trial are basic to Frost's thinking. Years later he was to repeat the argument of this poem in his play *A Masque of Reason* (1945). But "The Trial by Existence" is not a convincing poem—partly because this argument for an affirmative attitude to life is intrinsically implausible, and partly because it is presented in too didactic a way. In his later meditative poems Frost overcame both these drawbacks. In such poems as "Mending Wall," "Birches," and "West-Running Brook" the ideas are presented through the richer and subtler techniques of metaphor and symbol rather than through simple didactic exposition. And the ideas themselves are less abstract and moralistic. That sense of conflicting tensions that Frost was all too aware of in his life, and to which his pragmatism was a conscious answer, is explored in terms that are more human and practical.

In "Mending Wall" (1914) the central symbol of the wall acts as a focus for two conflicting attitudes.

Economically, it thus concentrates the poem's theme. The poem describes how each spring two farmers—the narrator and an older neighbor—meet at their property boundary to repair their common stone wall after the ravages of winter. The narrator questions the need for a wall at all, since he has an apple orchard and his neighbor pine trees:

> My apple trees will never get across
> And eat the cones under his pines, I tell him.

To this rationalizing, the old man simply retorts: "Good fences make good neighbors," and they go on constructing the barrier between them.

The balance of sympathy in the poem seems to rest with the narrator, and an inattentive reader might be led to assume that the poem simply advocates the abolition of walls. The narrator's argument is practical and sensible, his voice easygoing and tolerant. His common sense is based solidly on visible facts: "Something there is that doesn't love a wall." Yet he avoids defining the "something," though he makes this assertion twice. It is nothing so matter-of-fact, he claims, as "hunters," breaking the walls as they hunt for rabbits; nothing so fantastic as "elves," though he'd like to credit the old man with that kind of reasoning. The "something" is anthropomorphic, perhaps some principle of order in nature that denies any human attempt to impose limits on it; but the vagueness of definition contrasts oddly with the dogmatic order of the words—"Something there is." There is a certain equivocation here. It is as if real understanding lies beyond the pale of the speaker's rationalism.

The old man opposes this argument-by-empirical-fact with an argument-by-tradition. It too is an argument based on the practicalities of living. But he has inherited his country wisdom unthinkingly, never probing "behind his father's saying" to ask why good fences make good neighbors. To the speaker, he "moves in darkness" and seems "like an old-stone savage armed" as he places the rocks in position.

All reasonableness is on the narrator's side. Yet it is not ultimately convincing. Despite his good-humored condescension toward the old man, he continues with the job. In fact, it was he who initiated the wall mending ("I let my neighbor know beyond the hill"). Ultimately the poem would seem to be not so much about a simple conflict of attitude as about the different modes of thinking that inform both attitudes. Each of these modes—the purely empirical and the purely traditional—is found wanting. The conflict is deliberately unresolved, and the total effect of the poem is, ironically, more thoughtful and subtle, more true to human experience, than the effect of "Trial by Existence," in which Frost tried to justify the general conflicts of life by a simplistic account of their origin.

The equivocation in "Mending Wall" reflects Frost's own feeling. Whatever compunction he might have had at times, he would on the whole have opted for the principle of maintaining walls. When he was asked in 1959 to write a poem about the United Nations, he simply wrote the cynical couplet:

> Nature within her inmost self divides
> To trouble men with having to take sides.

He had no time for any philosophy that assumed that absolute harmony was possible or even desirable.

Something there is which insists on walls. He disapproved of the United Nations, regarding its concept of unity as arbitrary and artificial. The consciousness of individuality, the constructive tension between disparate elements, and the instinctual, intuitive interaction that he called "passionate preference"—these, for Frost, were the only viable premises for human action and creative thought. The function of a wall as a symbol, then, lies not in the fact that it shuts people off from each other ("Good fences make good neighbors") or that it may be rationally unnecessary ("Before I built a wall I'd ask to know / What I was walling in or walling out"), but that it focuses the constant tension of opposing elements, which Frost saw as the essence of the human condition.

Another symbol of this tension—as much a part of the realistic New England landscape as stone walls—is explored in "Birches" (1915). The starting point of this poem is the image of birch trees that are bending back toward the ground instead of continuing to grow upward. They are a common sight in New England, and Frost used them as a focus for ideas about emotional and intellectual ambivalence. The poem falls into three main divisions. After the introduction of the observed fact ("When I see birches bend to left and right / Across the lines of straighter darker trees") and a tentative statement of the speaker's fancy about the phenomenon ("I like to think some boy's been swinging them"), "Truth" breaks in "with all her matter of fact." The first section thus deals with the factual reason for the trees being bent. It is the winter ice storms that do it; the weight of the ice drags them down and "once they are bowed / So low for long, they never right themselves." So much for scientific "truth."

The second section reverts to the fanciful reason: "I should prefer to have some boy bend them." Yet this fancy still falls within the realm of factual possibility. Boys in New England do climb birch trees, carefully maintaining their "poise" till they reach the top, then kicking outward till the top branches bend and deposit them back on the ground. It is possible that constant "swinging" could make a tree permanently bent. The metaphorical implications of the imagined boy's actions are touched on, but not developed. He is seen as "subduing," "conquering," the birch trees, and learning the practicalities of "not launching out too soon," before the tree can bend with him. His climbing, particularly as he climbs higher and the tree starts to bend under his weight, requires him to keep a "poise" against the opposing pull of gravity, to strain the limits of natural laws:

> climbing carefully
> With the same pains you use to fill a cup
> Up to the brim, and even above the brim.

But it is not until the third section that the speaker develops the metaphor fully:

> So was I once myself a swinger of birches.
> And so I dream of going back to be.
>
> . . . .
>
> I'd like to get away from earth awhile
> And then come back to it and begin over.

The swinging of birches has become for him more than a childhood game. It is a metaphor for the ideal human attitude, finely balanced between a pragmatic acceptance of life as it is on earth and a sense of dissatisfaction with it:

> I'd like to go by climbing a birch tree,
> And climb black branches up a snow-white trunk
> *Toward* heaven, till the tree could bear no more,
> But dipped its top and set me down again.
> That would be good both going and coming back.

The climbing is partly a restorative escape (he only longs for it when he is "weary of considerations" and when "life is too much like a pathless wood") and partly spiritual aspiration (a climbing "toward heaven"). The two are not necessarily contradictory. Melville's Ishmael took to the sea with the same ambiguity of motive. But the important thing is the coming back. Frost's pragmatism is reflected in the gentle spoofing of all those classical myths, such as that of Tithonus, in which the gods perversely play havoc with man's aspirations. The speaker here prudently wants to have a bet both ways: "May no fate willfully misunderstand me / And half grant what I wish and snatch me away / Not to return." And his reasoning is equally pragmatic:

> ... Earth's the right place for love:
> I don't know where it's likely to go better.

It is a delightfully colloquial echo of Andrew Marvell's warning about the limitations of nonearthly existence:

> The grave's a fine and private place
> But none, I think, do there embrace.

The swinger of birches—as embodying a philosophical or ethical attitude—has had his critics. In an array of mixed metaphors, his conscious balance between "earth" and "heaven" has been seen as fence-sitting, drifting, or having his cake and eating it too.

The implication in such criticism is that a choice of one or the other, whatever inadequacies it might open up in terms of practical living, is a prerequisite for any claim to intellectual fiber. Yet Frost saw both art and life as "a bursting unity of opposites," and his insistence on holding contradictions in a deliberate tension, without seeking to resolve that tension, was a consciously adopted intellectual attitude, not an emotional slipperiness.

Indeed, Frost's position here is very close to Keats's "negative capability." Keats's clearest definition of this famous concept appeared in a letter to his brothers in 1817, written after a dinner party with some fashionable young men. For some time he had been pondering on the difference between minds that were incisive, intellectual, dogmatic (such as those of his dinner companions), and minds that were intuitive, passive, tentative; between, in other words, those who sought to arrive at a philosophical resolution or "goal" and those who believed that such a goal was at best tenuous, reachable only by "putting aside numerous objections." Walking home from that dinner, his ideas clarified themselves:

. . . several things dovetailed in my mind, and at once it struck me, what quality went to form a Man of Achievement especially in literature and which Shakespeare possessed so enormously—I mean *Negative Capability*, that is when man is capable of being in uncertainties, mysteries, doubts, without any irritable reaching after fact and reason.[7]

Keats's view of negative capability then, is that of a deliberately maintained equilibrium between emotion and the intellectual resolution of it, between "sensation" and "thought." The similarity to Frost's position is clear: the skepticism toward systematizing truth, the emphasis on sensation and intuition (what Frost called "passionate preference"), and above all the idea of balancing opposites in a deliberate tension—the conviction that ambiguities and contradictions not only cannot be resolved but that they ought not to be. Keats is interested in examining negative capability as an intellectual position. Frost is more concerned with achieving for himself a practical *modus vivendi*. But both view such tension as a creative force.

The swinger of birches thus embodies one of Frost's major themes. He represents a mode of consciously balancing the disparate forces of affirmation and negation that were captured as independent moods in many of the lyrics. Yet the balance, for him, is essentially an emotional one. The "voice" of the poem endorses this as the primary emphasis. Indeed, the casual throwaway quality of the last line ("One could do worse than be a swinger of birches") deliberately disclaims any intellectual pretension in his final attitude. It remains on the level of statement —whimsical, unexplored.

In "West-Running Brook" (1928), a similar theme is more intellectually examined by the main character; his emphasis is on an understanding of the tension of contraries rather than a simple acceptance of it as a way of life. A young married couple are looking at a brook that runs west when all the other brooks run east. The wife immediately sees this contrariety as relevant to their own human situation and as something vaguely creative, though she cannot explain her intuition: "It must be the brook / Can trust itself to go by contraries / The way I can with you—and you with me." But the brook offers a further symbol of contrariety, and the attempts to explain the nature and relevance of this are the crux of the poem. It is the wife who first notices the white foam that marks a point where the stream is thrown back on itself:

> "Look, look, it's waving to us with a wave
> To let us know it hears me."
>
>   "Why, my dear,
> That wave's been standing off this jut of shore—"
> (The black stream, catching on a sunken rock,
> Flung backward on itself in one white wave,
> And the white water rode the black forever,
> Not gaining but not losing, like a bird
> White feathers from the struggle of whose breast
> Flecked the dark stream and flecked the darker pool
> Below the point, and were at last driven wrinkled
> In a white scarf against the far-shore alders.)
> "That wave's been standing off this jut of shore
> Ever since rivers, I was going to say,
> Were made in heaven. It wasn't waved to us."
>
> "It wasn't, yet it was. If not to you,
> It was to me—in an annunciation."

The punctuation is important here in establishing three different perspectives to the symbol. To the wife, the phenomenon is seen only in terms of its personal relevance: it is a "wave" or, more importantly, an "annunciation," a private moment of revelation. Her husband's more realistic attitude is to disclaim such a personal interpretation of reality ("It wasn't waved to us"). Yet the "reality" of the phenomenon is not presented by him. It is the poet himself, intruding into the dialogue as he does only one other time in the poem, who gives us that, in the section deliberately marked off by parentheses. What he presents is the physical, visible fact—the stream, because of some sunken rocks, being "flung backward" on itself. Although he uses a simile to describe it ("like a bird") , the "fact" remains quite independent of any human analogy that may be drawn from it.

From the wife's "fancy" and the independent, observable fact the husband moves toward the understanding that forms the central passage of the poem:

> "Speaking of contraries, see how the brook
> In that white wave runs counter to itself.
> It is from that in water we were from
> Long, long before we were from any creature.
> Here we, in our impatience of the steps,
> Get back to the beginning of beginnings,
> The stream of everything that runs away.
> Some say existence like a Pirouot
> And Pirouette, forever in one place,
> Stands still and dances, but it runs away;
> It seriously, sadly, runs away
> To fill the abyss's void with emptiness.
> It flows beside us in this water brook,
> But it flows over us. It flows between us
> To separate us for a panic moment.
> It flows between us, over us, and *with* us.
> And it is time, strength, tone, light, life, and love—
> And even substance lapsing unsubstantial;
> The universal cataract of death
> That spends to nothingness—and unresisted,
> Save by some strange resistance in itself,
> Not just a swerving, but a throwing back,
> As if regret were in it and were sacred.

. . . .

It is this backward motion toward the source,
Against the stream, that most we see ourselves in,
The tribute of the current to the source.
It is from this in nature we are from.
It is most us."

The west-running brook is seen as the flow of existence moved inexorably by time toward decay. It is the oldest of metaphors—life seen as a stream or voyage. But the emphasis here is wholly negative. The brook is the symbol of "existence" that "seriously, sadly, runs away / To fill the abyss's void with emptiness." It is the "universal cataract of death / That spends to nothingness." It flows to no Elysian fields, no Heraclitean flux, no Christian heaven. The whole inexorable process would seem pointless and sadly deterministic were it not for that "strange resistance in itself" by which the water is thrown back toward the source. That small but brave resistance to the general flow becomes for the husband a symbol of independence, of positive assertion, of everything that gives meaning to life. Its "contrariety" is thus, in the broadest sense, creative. He sees it as a paradigm of our human identity, disengaging itself from the overwhelming flow of existence and asserting its independent meaning.

The terms of this human identity are vaguely religious—the memory of a lost Eden perhaps ("a throwing back, / As if regret were in it and were sacred"), or the instinctive worship of a Creator ("The tribute of the current to the source"). But Frost's position here is once again more existential than orthodox. Orthodoxy would have given a clearer direction, a more definite goal, to the general flow of the brook. Here the emphasis is less on the brook than

on that stubborn resistance to it that seems "most us."
The meaning of our human lives finds definition
through a constantly maintained balance, "not gaining but not losing," between opposing tensions. "West-
Running Brook" thus gives a more intellectual extension to that sense of equipoise that Frost examined
in "Mending Wall" and "Birches."

Finally, let us look at a poem that is in many ways
the pinnacle of Frost's achievement as a poet—"Directive" (1946). It is perhaps the most fully realized of
all his poems. It is one in which theme is inseparable
from symbol, tone, rhythm, and structure, and one in
which so many of the Frostian themes reach a kind of
culmination: the existential loneliness, the self-defin-
ing resistance to the engulfing flow of existence, the
individual salvation that is partly given (through the
redemptive waters of the "source" described in the
poem) and partly earned (through the Grail-like
goblet that had been so deliberately set aside). Yet it is
a poem that has been largely overlooked, though both
Reuben Brower[8] and Theodore Morrison[9] have offered excellent analyses of it.

In a sense "Directive" takes up where "West-
Running Brook" left off. It is a journey back up the
"universal cataract of death," a step beyond that stoic
point where human identity bravely holds its own,
"not gaining but not losing," against the annihilating
tide; a step beyond the tension of contrariety to an
original source. It is Frost's only attempt at some
reconciliation of that conscious ambivalence that he
maintained so deliberately in so many of his poems.
The last line of this poem—"Drink and be whole
again beyond confusion"—has none of the defensive
whimsy of "One could do worse than be a swinger of

birches." The calm solemnity of tone is almost biblical.

"Directive" describes a journey that begins in a world of confusion and decay, and progresses, through various "serial ordeals" that echo the quests of Arthurian romance and the paradoxes of the Christian mystics, to a state "beyond confusion."

> Back out of all this now too much for us,
> Back in a time made simple by the loss
> Of detail, burned, dissolved, and broken off
> Like graveyard marble sculpture in the weather,
> There is a house that is no more a house
> Upon a farm that is no more a farm
> And in a town that is no more a town.
> The road there, if you'll let a guide direct you
> Who only has at heart your getting lost,
> May seem as if it should have been a quarry—
> Great monolithic knees the former town
> Long since gave up pretense of keeping covered.
> And there's a story in a book about it:
> Besides the wear of iron wagon wheels
> The ledges show lines ruled southeast-northwest,
> The chisel work of an enormous Glacier
> That braced his feet against the Arctic Pole.
> You must not mind a certain coolness from him
> Still said to haunt this side of Panther Mountain.
> Nor need you mind the serial ordeal
> Of being watched from forty cellar holes
> As if by eye pairs out of forty firkins.
> As for the woods' excitement over you
> That sends light rustle rushes to their leaves,
> Charge that to upstart inexperience.
> Where were they all not twenty years ago?
> They think too much of having shaded out
> A few old pecker-fretted apple trees.
> Make yourself up a cheering song of how

Someone's road home from work this once was,
Who may be just ahead of you on foot
Or creaking with a buggy load of grain.
The height of the adventure is the height
Of country where two village cultures faded
Into each other. Both of them are lost.
And if you're lost enough to find yourself
By now, pull in your ladder road behind you
And put a sign up CLOSED to all but me.
Then make yourself at home. The only field
Now left's no bigger than a harness gall.
First there's the children's house of make-believe,
Some shattered dishes underneath a pine,
The playthings in the playhouse of the children.
Weep for what little things could make them glad.
Then for the house that is no more a house,
But only a belilaced cellar hole,
Now slowly closing like a dent in dough.
This was no playhouse but a house in earnest.
Your destination and your destiny's
A brook that was the water of the house,
Cold as a spring as yet so near its source,
Too lofty and original to rage.
(We know the valley streams that when aroused
Will leave their tatters hung on barb and thorn.)
I have kept hidden in the instep arch
Of an old cedar at the waterside
A broken drinking goblet like the Grail
Under a spell so the wrong ones can't find it,
So can't get saved, as Saint Mark says they mustn't.
(I stole the goblet from the children's playhouse.)
Here are your waters and your watering place.
Drink and be whole again beyond confusion.

The present world which is the starting point of
the poem is not "too much with us" but "too much
for us." How subtly Frost modifies and extends the

Wordsworthian echo here. His phrasing, after what we have already noted in his themes about the creative value of some tension of contrariety, implies a flabby lack of challenge—the world is too much *for* us. At the same time, its colloquial sense—as in "It's all too much for me"—reinforces the impression of spiritual defeatism.

The journey is "back . . . back": past individual life ("graveyard marble sculpture"); past a Whitmanesque identification with others who have lived on the same earth ("Who may be just ahead of you on foot / Or creaking with a buggy load of grain"); past the "upstart" reclamation of one's human traces by Nature, which has overgrown the apple orchards that man had long ago won from her; past even the marks of geological change in which the "road" is described as following a "ledge" that was "The chisel work of an enormous Glacier / That braced his feet against the Arctic Pole"; and back beyond the anthropomorphic world of myth ("him / Still said to haunt this side of Panther Mountain").

The speaker maintains an assured colloquiality. He addresses most of the poem to "you," but the "you" slips so easily into "I" at the end that it is obvious the two are integral. The "you" form makes the total effect less personal perhaps, but more importantly it establishes an easy colloquial tone, jaunty, chatty ("Make yourself up a cheering song"; "Pull in your ladder road behind you"). The only other "character" in the poem is a "guide"—if you'll let him direct you—who also blends so easily into the "you" and the "I" that he may be seen as a kind of alter ego of both the reader and the poet.

The journey is fraught with the paradoxes that

beleaguer most quest myths. The guide "only has at
heart your getting lost." The apparent destination—
"There is a house"—is immediately negated—"that
is no more a house." And just when the "height of
the adventure" is reached—a high place where two
village cultures once faded into each other—we are
deflated by the statement that "Both of them are
lost." But the resolution of all this paradox is not the
orthodox salvation-through-surrender idea, losing
one's life in order to save it; that would be too
clichéd altogether for this highly individualized
poem.

Having reached this graveyard of lost cultures,
"you" are urged by the guide to "make yourself at
home," but only if you are "lost enough to find yourself"; and your salvation there is to be an oddly un-
sharable one ("pull in your ladder road behind you /
And put a sign up CLOSED to all but me.") And
what then? The scene that confronts you now is at
once homely and apocalyptic. The field, "no bigger
than a harness gall," mocks, through this image, the
pitiful attempt once made to harness it; it is now
simply a small scar on the landscape. The house—
"no more a house, / But only a belilaced cellar hole, /
Now slowly closing like a dent in dough"—is mocked
by the survival of "the children's house of make-
believe." The only relics of your former life there are
"some shattered dishes," the hieroglyphics of your
identity.

But the "house"—your futile barrier against
the flux of time—is not, after all, to be your journey's
end. Instead:

> Your destination and your destiny's
> A brook that was the water of the house.

This, then, is the center of the poem—the stream
that once fed the house (and "house" begins to take
on the biblical sense of "genealogy"). It is described
in terms reminiscent of the source of religious or
poetic inspiration in Greek myths—"lofty and original"—and its waters are now redemptive.

At least they are potentially redemptive. Finding them is not enough. You must drink them, and
from a strange chalice, broken and stolen from
childhood:

> I have kept hidden in the instep arch
> Of an old cedar at the waterside
> A broken drinking goblet like the Grail
> Under a spell so the wrong ones can't find it,
> So can't get saved, as Saint Mark says they mustn't.
> (I stole the goblet from the children's playhouse.)
> Here are your waters and your watering place.
> Drink and be whole again beyond confusion.

The key to this passage and to the meaning of
the goblet is in the reference to Saint Mark. In
Chapter 4, verses 10–12, immediately after the parable of the sower and the seed, Mark records:

And when he was alone, they that were about him with the
twelve asked of him the parable. And he said unto them,
Unto you it is given to know the mystery of the kingdom of
God: but unto them that are without, all these things are
done in parables: That seeing they may see, and not per-
ceive; and hearing they may hear, and not understand; lest
at any time they should be converted, and their sins should
be forgiven them.

Theodore Morrison has noted that Frost was
fascinated by the paradox implicit in these verses.
They seem to suggest that Christ talked in parables

not, as we generally assume, so that everyone can
understand, but in order to prevent the uninitiated
from understanding. Frost likened this notion of the
exclusiveness of truth—something that has to be
worked for—to poetry and made continual reference
to it in conversation and lecture. It appealed not so
much perhaps to the streak of the Puritan in Frost
(akin though it is to the Puritan concept of "elec-
tion") as to his Yankee independence. Not everyone
who approaches the waters of truth can be saved—
nor should they be, Frost would argue. A man should
be responsible for his own "wholeness": that is his
challenge and his glory.

Working from the notes that Hyde Cox made of
Frost's conversations about "Directive," Morrison
quotes:

In the midst of this 'now too much for us he tells everyone
to go back . . . to whatever source they have. The source
might even be a conventional religion. . . . but religion is
most of all valuable when something original has been contributed to it. . . .

It would be the poet's directive that one must go back
to what he believes in his heart to be the source; and to
the extent that he has saved something aside, removed from
worldly experience—unpolluted, he would be able to con-
tribute something himself.[10]

The stolen goblet, hidden in the tabernacle-like
tree beside the source, is thus preserved as a frag-
ment of lost innocence, an intimation of immortality.
But there still remains the vexing question: why is
it "broken"? Why is it such a parody of the real
Grail? What it suggests is that Frost's view of
human capacity is infinitely sadder than that of
Malory. The symbols, emphasizing as they do the

limitations of our spiritual questing, are almost un-
bearably poignant. Even here at the source the ritual
gestures are games of hide-and-seek and casting a
"spell"; the Grail is a broken plaything from the playhouse of the children, three times removed from any
Platonic concept of reality. The oracular solemnity
of the last two lines ("Here are your waters and
your watering place. / Drink and be whole again
beyond confusion") is somehow undercut by the gestures, even the rhythm, of the preceding lines. Salvation is possible, and it is earned by those who
have something of their own to bring to its healing
waters. But we move toward it in solitude, working
only with shattered hieroglyphics from a world of
make-believe, fragments shored against our ruin.

Ultimately, any attempt to explain the "meaning" of this poem belittles it. Its real power is emotional, drawn from the rich resonance of its sparse
narrative. The Arthurian echoes combine with a certain fairy-tale incantation ("There is a house that is
no more a house / Upon a farm that is no more a
farm") to give it the dimension of myth. At the same
time the colloquial voice of the guide ("pull in your
ladder road behind you . . . make yourself at home")
anchors it to the realities of individual experience.
Indeed, the sureness with which all the literary
echoes in the poem—biblical, Arthurian, Wordsworthian—are interwoven shows that Frost could match
Eliot in the business of ironic analogy. In "Directive," Frost achieves a poetic integration of theme
and form that makes it one of his finest poems.

Throughout this brief examination of some of
Frost's major themes, we have seen that, despite his
reputation as a nature poet, his concerns are essen-

tially human ones. In a very real sense he is a philosophical poet. Nature simply provided him with a
constant metaphor—the "fact" with which his imagination could work. Certainly it provided no haven
for him; Frost's characters move in a terrible loneliness. In one of his bleakest poems, "The Most of It"
(1942), Frost presents a man alone in a wilderness
who hears merely the echo of his own voice when he
"would cry out on life." What he wanted was
"counter-love, original response." At length he hears
what might be an answer from nature—something
crashing through the cliff's talus on the other side
of the lake, splashing into the water, swimming
across, and then:

> As a great buck it powerfully appeared,
> Pushing the crumpled water up ahead,
> And landed pouring like a waterfall,
> And stumbled through the rocks with horny tread,
> And forced the underbrush—and that was all.

"That was all." The great buck has associations with
Yeats's apocalyptic beast "slouching towards Bethle-
hem," yet it is somehow lonelier and more pointless,
its sheer indifference a mockery of the "counter-
love" the man so earnestly cried out for. "That was
all." But not quite "all." Rather "the most of it."
There is still the man himself. It is his imagination
that creates the ultimate meaning of the scene and
the poem. At its best nature may offer momentary
revelations of truth ("For Once, Then, Something");
at its worst, merely a travesty of man's expectations
("The Most of It"). More often, it simply provides
analogies, correspondences, "facts." It is man's imagination that makes them humanly relevant.

Frost has his limitations as a thinker. Even in his definition of a poem as a "momentary stay against confusion," there is an implication that whatever meaning can be thus won is accidental and transitory. His intellectual preoccupations are disparate, not welded into any coherent structure. His moral values—concerned with consciously maintaining a perpetual cold war between affirmation and negation—make for an unglamorous stability rather than a tragic grandeur, for adjustment rather than confrontation.

In spite of all this, there is something reassuringly sane and unpretentious about Frost's thematic concerns. If he fails to explore the heart of darkness it is because he has come close enough to it to be wary of entering in. His acceptance of life on its own terms represents an affirmation that was won at the cost of bitter personal negations, and it rarely becomes complacent. There is an intellectual rigor behind the often whimsical irresolution of its expression. Frost held his irresolution deliberately. To say this is not to make it automatically a viable philosophical position. It *may* be "spiritual drifting." But, bearing in mind the consistency of such ideas in Frost's poetry, their hard-headed practicality, and the stern discipline of metaphor and symbol through which they are examined, this seems too glib a charge.

Notes

1. Introduction . . . Mostly Biographical

1. Unpublished letter from Robert Frost to Lewis N. Chase, 11 July 1917. Now in Library of Congress.
2. Lawrance Thompson, ed., *Selected Letters of Robert Frost* (New York: Holt, Rinehart & Winston, 1964), p. 25.
3. Louis Untermeyer, ed., *The Letters of Robert Frost to Louis Untermeyer* (New York: Holt, Rinehart & Winston, 1963), p. 191.
4. Unpublished letter from Robert Frost to Lewis N. Chase, 29 April 1917. Now in Library of Congress.
5. Robert Frost, Introduction to *King Jasper*, by Edwin Arlington Robinson (New York: Macmillan, 1935). Introduction reprinted in *Selected Prose of Robert Frost*, ed. Hyde Cox and Edward Connery Lathem (New York: Holt, Rinehart & Winston, 1966), p. 67.
6. Ibid., p. 65.
7. Untermeyer, *Letters*, p. 166.
8. Ibid.

2. The Lyric Voice

1. Robert Frost, "The Figure a Poem Makes," in *Selected Prose of Robert Frost*, ed. Hyde Cox and Edward Connery Lathem (New York: Holt, Rinehart & Winston, 1966), p. 18.
2. Louis Untermeyer, ed., *The Letters of Robert Frost to Louis Untermeyer* (New York: Holt, Rinehart & Winston, 1963), pp. 75–76.
3. Lawrance Thompson, ed., *Selected Letters of Robert Frost* (New York: Holt, Rinehart & Winston, 1964), p. 80.
4. Ibid., p. 128.
5. Lawrance Thompson, *Robert Frost: The Early Years* (New York: Holt, Rinehart & Winston, 1966), pp. 152–53.
6. Frost, "The Figure a Poem Makes," in *Selected Prose*, p. 19.
7. Lionel Trilling, "A Speech on Robert Frost: A Cultural Episode," in *Robert Frost: A Collection of Critical Essays*, ed. James M. Cox (Englewood Cliffs, N.J.: Prentice-Hall, 1962), p. 157.
8. Lawrance Thompson, *The Early Years*, p. 512.

3. The Dramatic Narrative

1. Unpublished letter from Robert Frost to Lewis N. Chase, 29 April 1917. Now in Library of Congress.
2. Lawrance Thompson, ed., *Selected Letters of Robert Frost* (New York: Holt, Rinehart & Winston, 1964), p. 80.
3. Quoted by Robert Newdick, "Robert Frost and the Sound of Sense," *American Literature* 9 (November 1937):298.
4. Thompson, *Selected Letters*, p. 107.
5. Ibid.

6. Robert Frost, "Preface to *A Way Out*," in *Selected Prose of Robert Frost*, ed. Hyde Cox and Edward Connery Lathem (New York: Holt, Rinehart & Winston, 1966), p. 13.

7. Thompson, *Selected Letters*, p. 182.

8. Unpublished letter from Robert Frost to F. S. Flint, 6 July 1913. Now in University of Texas Library.

9. Thompson, *Selected Letters*, p. 180.

10. Quoted in *A Treasury of the Theatre*, ed. John Gassner (New York: Simon & Schuster, 1959), p. 265.

11. Thompson, *Selected Letters*, p. 182.

4. Frost and the Sonnet Form

1. Unpublished letter from Robert Frost to Lewis N. Chase, 11 July 1917. Now in Library of Congress.

2. Lawrance Thompson, ed., *Selected Letters of Robert Frost* (New York: Holt, Rinehart & Winston, 1964), pp. 418–19.

3. Robert Frost, "Education by Poetry," in *Selected Prose of Robert Frost*, ed. Hyde Cox and Edward Connery Lathem (New York: Holt, Rinehart & Winston, 1966), p. 36.

4. Analogy made in conversation. Quoted in Reginald Cook, *The Dimensions of Robert Frost* (New York: Holt, Rinehart & Winston, 1958). Reprinted by Barnes and Noble, 1968, p. 139.

5. Frost, "Education by Poetry," in *Selected Prose*, p. 41.

6. Frost, "The Constant Symbol," in *Selected Prose*, p. 26.

7. Ibid., p. 27.

8. Manuscript in the Huntington Library, San Marino, California. Quoted in Lawrance Thompson, *Robert Frost: The Early Years* (New York: Holt, Rinehart & Winston, 1966), p. 582.

9. Frost, "The Poetry of Amy Lowell," in *Selected Prose*, pp. 71–72.

5. *The Meditative Voice . . . Some Major Themes*

1. Lawrance Thompson, ed., *Selected Letters of Robert Frost* (New York: Holt, Rinehart & Winston, 1964), p. 343.
2. Ibid., pp. 324–25.
3. William James, "Is Life Worth Living?" in *The Will to Believe, and Other Essays in Popular Philosophy* (New York: Dover, 1956), p. 59. Original publication, 1897.
4. Ibid., p. 60.
5. Thompson, *Selected Letters*, p. 369.
6. Ibid., pp. 417–18.
7. John Keats, *The Letters of John Keats 1814–1821*, Vol. 1, ed. Hyder E. Rollins (Cambridge: Harvard University Press, 1958), p. 193.
8. See Reuben Brower, *The Poetry of Robert Frost: Constellations of Intention* (New York: Oxford University Press, 1963), pp. 232–42.
9. See Theodore Morrison, "The Agitated Heart," *The Atlantic Monthly*, July 1967, pp. 77–79.
10. Ibid., p. 79.

Bibliography

1. *Works by Frost*

POETRY

A Boy's Will. London: David Nutt, 1913. New York, Henry Holt, 1915.

North of Boston. London: David Nutt, 1914. New York, Henry Holt, 1915.

Mountain Interval. New York: Henry Holt, 1916.

New Hampshire. New York: Henry Holt, 1923.

West-Running Brook. New York: Henry Holt, 1928.

A Further Range. New York: Henry Holt, 1936.

A Witness Tree. New York: Henry Holt, 1942.

A Masque of Reason. New York: Henry Holt, 1945.

A Masque of Mercy. New York: Henry Holt, 1947.

Steeple Bush. New York: Henry Holt, 1947.

In the Clearing. New York: Holt, Rinehart & Winston, 1962.

The standard collection is *The Poetry of Robert Frost*, ed. Edward Connery Lathem. New York: Holt, Rinehart & Winston, 1969.

PROSE WRITINGS

Cox, Hyde, and Lathem, Edward Connery, eds. *Selected Prose of Robert Frost*. New York: Holt, Rinehart & Winston, 1966.

Lathem, Edward Connery, ed. *Interviews with Robert Frost*. New York: Holt, Rinehart & Winston, 1966.

Thompson, Lawrance, ed. *Selected Letters of Robert Frost*. New York: Holt, Rinehart & Winston, 1964.

Untermeyer, Louis, ed. *The Letters of Robert Frost to Louis Untermeyer*. New York: Holt, Rinehart & Winston, 1963.

2. *Works about Frost*

BIBLIOGRAPHIES

Clymer, W. B. Shubrick, and Green, Charles R. *Robert Frost: A Bibliography*. Amherst: The Jones Library, 1937.

Mertins, Louis and Esther. *The Intervals of Robert Frost: A Critical Bibliography*. Berkeley: University of California Press, 1947.

BIOGRAPHIES

Cox, Sidney. *A Swinger of Birches*. New York: New York University Press, 1957.

Mertins, Louis. *Robert Frost: Life and Talks-Walking*. Norman: University of Oklahoma Press, 1965.

Thompson, Lawrance. *Robert Frost: The Early Years, 1874–1915*. New York: Holt, Rinehart & Winston, 1966.
———. *Robert Frost: The Years of Triumph, 1915–1938*. New York: Holt, Rinehart & Winston, 1970.

CRITICAL MATERIAL

Books

Brower, Reuben. *The Poetry of Robert Frost: Constellations of Intention*. New York: Oxford University Press, 1963.

Cook, Reginald L. *The Dimensions of Robert Frost.* New York: Rinehart, 1959.

Cox, James M., ed. *Robert Frost: A Collection of Critical Essays.* Englewood Cliffs, N. J.: Prentice-Hall, 1962.

Isaacs, Elizabeth. *An Introduction to Robert Frost.* Denver: Alan Swallow, 1962.

Squires, Radcliffe. *The Major Themes of Robert Frost.* Ann Arbor: University of Michigan Press, 1963.

Thompson, Lawrance. *Fire and Ice: The Art and Thought of Robert Frost.* New York: Henry Holt & Co., 1942.

Thornton, Richard, ed. *Recognition of Robert Frost.* New York: Henry Holt, 1937.

Articles and Essays

Beach, Joseph Warren. "Robert Frost." *Yale Review* 43 (Winter 1954):204–217.

Carlson, Eric W. "Robert Frost on 'Vocal Imagination': The Merger of Form and Content." *American Literature* 33 (January 1962):519–22.

Ciardi, John. "Robert Frost: The Way to the Poem." *Saturday Review* 41 (12 April 1958):13–15, 65.

Cook, Reginald L. "Frost on Frost: The Making of Poems." *American Literature* 28 (March 1956):62–72.

Cox, Sidney. "The Courage to Be New: A Reappraisal of Robert Frost." *Vermont History* 22 (April 1954):119–26.

Cowley, Malcolm. "Frost: A Dissenting Opinion." *New Republic* 3 (11 and 18 September 1944):312–13, 345–47.

Montgomery, Marion. "Robert Frost and His Use of Barriers: Man vs. Nature toward God." *South Atlantic Quarterly* 57 (Summer 1958):339–53.

Mulder, William. "Freedom and Form: Robert Frost's Double Discipline." *South Atlantic Quarterly* 54 (July 1955):386–93.

Newdick, Robert S. "Robert Frost and the Sound of Sense." *American Literature* 9 (November 1937):289–300.

———. "Robert Frost and the Dramatic." *New England Quarterly* 10 (June 1937):263–69.

Newdick, Robert S. "Robert Frost's Other Harmony."
   Sewanee Review 48 (July–September 1940):409–418.
O'Donnell, William G. "Robert Frost and New England:
   A Revaluation." *Yale Review* 37 (Summer 1948):698–
   712.
Poirier, Richard. "Robert Frost." *Paris Review*, No. 24
   (Summer-Fall 1960) , pp. 88–120.
Waggoner, Hyatt Howe. "The Humanistic Idealism of
   Robert Frost." *American Literature* 13 (November
   1941):207–233.
Winters, Yvor. "Robert Frost, or The Spiritual Drifter as
   Poet." *Sewanee Review* 56 (Autumn 1948):564–96.

Index

Abercrombie, Lascelles, 7
"Acquainted with the
        Night," 21, 34, 80, 102
Affirmation of life, 33–34,
        102, 103, 108, 109, 129
"After Apple Picking," 57
Agnosticism, and philosophy
        of life, 105
"Aim Was Song, The," 21
Ambiguity and ambivalence,
        use of, 26, 36, 42, 56,
        76, 120
Amherst College, 8
    and student newspaper,
        81, 105
Anthropomorphism, use of,
        39–40, 110
Argument from design, 89
Arnold, Matthew, as prophet
        of doom, 106
Arthurian legend, in "Direc-
        tive," 121, 126, 127

As I Lay Dying (Faulkner),
        13
Autobiographical elements,
        32, 39, 62–63, 71
    from courtship days, 30
    from marriage, 6, 9, 40–
        41, 78

"Bartleby" (Melville), 101,
        103
Bartlett, John, correspond-
        ence with, 49
"Bereft," 29–33, 39–40, 56,
        102
"Birches," 13, 109, 112–14,
        116, 120
Black comedy, 13, 68
Blake, William, 42, 83, 108
Blank verse, 78
Book of Thel (Blake), 108
Boston Evening Transcript
        (newspaper), 8

Boy's Will, A, 6, 7, 22, 25, 40, 44, 52, 106
Braithwaite, William, 8
Bridges, Robert, 50–51
Brower, Reuben, 120
Browning, Robert, influence of, 62, 78

Cambridge University, 10
Characterization, 11–12, 13, 16, 63–64
Chase, Lewis, correspondence with, 12, 80
Chekhov, Anton, influence of, 54–55, 60
Coleridge, Samuel, 83
"Come In," 13, 26–29, 32, 102
Contrast, use of, 57–58
Cox, Hyde, 126
Cox, Sidney, correspondence with, 51
Criticism of Frost, 5, 33, 100

Dartmouth College, 4, 5, 8, 30
"Death of a Hired Man, The," 51, 54
"Desert Places," 34
"Design," 16, 32, 34, 80, 85, 88–94, 101
Dickinson, Emily, 2, 34
"Directive," 2, 8, 13, 120-27
Donne, John, 95
"Dramatic eclogues," 52–53
Dramatic poetry, 54, 78
  "dramas," 54, 70–71

dramatic monologues, 54, 62, 63–64, 67
  "static" dramas, 54, 55–56, 60
"Drumlin Woodchuck, A," 60, 102
"Dust of Snow," 32

Eliot, T. S.
  compared to Frost, 5, 78, 80–81, 100, 101, 127
  as prophet of doom, 105
Elizabethan poetry, 94, 95
Emerson, Ralph Waldo, and Frost's philosophy, 83, 101, 102, 104, 109
England, life in, 6–7

Faulkner, William, 13, 60
"Fear, The," 37, 54, 71–75, 78
"Felt experience" (Leavis), concept of, 81
"Figure a Poem Makes, The," 32
Fin-de-siècle poetry, 23, 48
Flint, F. S., 7
  correspondence with, 53
Folk comedy, tradition of, 13, 68
"For Once, Then, Something," 12, 128
Free verse, Frost's views on, 25, 81
Frost, Carol (son), 8, 80
Frost, Elinor White (wife)
  and courtship, 3–4, 5, 30

and marriage, 6, 9, 40–41,
    78
Frost, Irma (daughter), 80
Frost, Isabelle (mother), 3
Frost, Jean (sister), 3, 8, 80
Frost, Robert
    education of, at Dart-
        mouth College, 4, 5,
        30
    education of, at Lawrence
        High School, 3–4
    education of, at Harvard
        University, 5, 103
    and family life, 6, 8–9, 80
    honors received by, 10
    literary career of, 6–8, 9–
        10
    and marriage, 5–6, 9, 78
    personality of, 2, 8, 9, 80
    teaching career of, 4, 5, 6,
        8
    and views on education, 5
    youth of, 3–4

Georgians, 7
Gibson, Wilfred, 7

Hamlet (Shakespeare), 103
Harvard University, 5, 8, 103
Hawthorne, Nathaniel, 2, 34
"Hill Wife, The," 36–40, 65
"Home Burial," 6, 7, 51, 54,
    75–78
Honorary doctorates, 10
"House Fear," 37, 38–39
"Housekeeper, The," 53
Hulme, T. E., 7

Humor, 13, 14–15, 29, 60, 68,
    70
"Hyla Brook," 32, 103, 107

Imagery, examples of, 23, 24,
    41–42, 90–91, 92, 93,
    112
Imagist movement, 7, 61
"Impulse, The," 37, 40
Independent, The (newspa-
    per), 6
Innovations in poetic form,
    16–17, 34, 36–37, 71,
    78, 85
"Into My Own," 5, 27
"In White," 93–94
Irony, use of, 13, 15, 36, 44,
    49, 111, 127
"Is Life Worth Living?"
    (William James), 104,
    108–109

James, Henry, 2, 34, 71
James, William, influence
    of, 103–105, 108–109
Juxtaposition, use of, 29, 58,
    73–74, 75

Keats, John, 27–28, 115–16
Kennedy, John F., inaugura-
    tion of, 10
King Jasper (Robinson), 14,
    20

Leavis, F. R., 81
"Lesson for Today, The,"
    106

Letters of Frost, 2, 7
"Loneliness: Her Word,"
        37–38
"Lovely Shall Be Choosers,
        The," 3
Lowell, Amy, 8, 54
Lyric poetry, 21, 32, 34, 36–
        37, 44–45
    and "The Hill Wife," 37
    and "Reluctance," 22, 23,
        24–25

Macbeth (Shakespeare), 91
Maeterlinck, Maurice, and
        "static" drama, 54–55,
        56
Malory, Thomas, 126
Marvell, Andrew, 114
Masque of Reason, A, 109
Masters, Edgar Lee, 20
Meditative poems, 100, 101
"Meeting and Passing," 54,
        60–62, 80
Melville, Herman, 2, 34
    and "Bartleby," 101–102,
        103
    and *Moby Dick*, 35, 36,
        90–91, 114
"Mending Wall," 7, 11–12,
        109–112, 120
Metaphor, use of, 24, 27, 98,
        107, 113–14, 119, 128
    in sonnets, 86, 87–88, 89,
        95–96, 97
Metaphysical poetry, 95, 96
Milton, John, sonnets of, 86

Moby Dick (Melville), 35,
        36, 114
Moral stance, in poetry, 68,
        70
Moral values of Frost, 129
Morrison, Theodore, 120,
        125–26
"Most of It, The," 2, 54, 128
"Mountain, The," 10–11
Mountain Interval, 56
"Mowing," 80, 103, 106
Munch, Edvard, 35
Music, use of, 21, 22–23
"My Butterfly," 6

Naturalism, 109
"Negative capability"
        (Keats), concept of,
        115–16
"Neither Out Far Nor In
        Deep," 16, 33–37, 101
New England
    influence of, on poetry, 3,
        17
    literary tradition of, 2, 34
    as setting, 53, 112–13
New Hampshire, life in,
        5–6
Nitchie, George, and criti-
        cism of Frost, 5
North of Boston, 7, 25, 52,
        53, 62

"Objective correlative"
        (Eliot), concept of, 81
"Ode to a Nightingale"
        (Keats), 27–28

"Oft-Repeated Dream, The,"
37, 39–40
"Old Man's Winter Night,
An," 54, 56–60, 61, 62
"Once by the Pacific," 80
"Onset, The," 102
"Our Hold on the Planet,"
102
"Oven Bird, The," 32, 80
Oxford University, 10

Paradox, use of, 87, 89, 90,
96, 97, 123–24, 125–26
Parallels, use of, 85, 86, 88,
89
Parody, 12, 43–44, 126
"Pauper Witch of Grafton,
The," 54, 68–70
Persona, 11–12, 14–15, 16,
23, 24, 26–27, 28, 37,
50, 52, 61
Pessimism, 102
Petrarchan sonnet, 89
Philosophy of Frost, on life,
105. *See also* Affirma-
tion of life;
Pragmatism
Philosophy of Frost, on
poetry
and "belief," 15
and "clarification of life,"
11, 20, 82, 98
and conceptualization, 11
conservatism of, 20
and creative process, 14,
25–26, 83–84
development of, 6, 7

and drama, 51–52
and form, 20–21, 80–82,
82–83
and humor, 14–15
and metaphor, 82
and music, 21
and "performance," 11, 82
and persona, *see* Persona
and "the sound of sense,"
48–49
and tension, 25–26
and ulteriority, 98
and way of "saying a
thing," 11, 13
Plays by Frost, 51
Poe, Edgar Allan, 90–91
Porcupine, The (Robinson),
51–52
Pound, Ezra, 6, 7
Pragmatism, 15–16, 101,
105–106, 109, 114
as theme, 44, 60, 103, 107
"Provide, Provide," 42–44
Public image of Frost, 2, 5,
6, 8, 10, 33–34, 100
Pulitzer Prizes, 8
Puritan concept, in "Directive," 126
"Putting in the Seed," 80,
85–88, 94, 95

"Range-Finding," 80
"Reluctance," 21, 22–25, 26,
29, 34
Rembrandt, 55
"Road Not Taken, The," 2,
12, 21

*Robert Frost: The Early
    Years* (Thompson), 2
*Robert Frost: The Years of
    Triumph* (Thompson), 2
Robinson, Edwin Arlington,
    14, 15, 20, 51–52, 74

Saint Mark, gospel of, and
    "Directive," 125
Satire, use of, 44
"Self-reliance," concept of,
    104
"Servant to Servants, A," 7,
    37, 54, 62–67, 70
Shakespeare, William, 91,
    103, 115
    sonnets of, 80, 84, 86
"Silken Tent, The," 80, 85,
    94–97
"Smile, The," 37, 39
"Snow," 51
Sonnets, 80, 98
    Elizabethan, 95
    Petrarchan, 89
    Shakespearean, 86
Spoon River Anthology
    (Masters), 20
Stevens, Wallace, 5, 101
"Stolen Child, The" (Yeats),
    23
"Stopping by Woods," 2, 11,
    21, 27
Stranger, The (Camus), 34
"Subverted Flower, The," 2,
    40–42
Symbolist poetry, 34

Symbols, use of, 56–57, 73,
    85, 109–110, 117, 119,
    126–27

Technique, 13, 25, 26, 31–32
    and colloquialism, 31–32,
        58, 70, 85–86, 90, 123
    and dramatic monologue,
        37–39
    and meter, 26, 28–29, 31–
        32, 44, 83–84, 86
    and "realism," 62–63
    and repetition, 31, 35, 58
    and rhyme, 23, 31, 89
    and rhythm, 25, 29, 97
    and "sound," 16, 21, 48
    and "sound of sense," 25,
        49, 67, 69, 74, 78
    and speaking voice, 12–13,
        21, 24–25, 34, 48–49,
        100
    and tension, 28
    and "tune," 21, 45, 52
    and visual effect, 61, 62, 73
    and "voice," 16–17, 44–45,
        58–59
    See also Ambiguity and
        ambivalence, use of;
        Anthropomorphism,
        use of; Characteriza-
        tion; Contrast, use of;
        Folk comedy, tradi-
        tion of; Imagery,
        examples of; Innova-
        tions in poetic form;
        Irony, use of; Juxta-
        position, use of;

Metaphor, use of;
Music, use of; Para-
dox, use of; Parallels,
use of; Persona; Phi-
losophy of Frost, on
poetry; Symbols, use
of
Themes, 5, 9
of "caring," 75
of conflict, 76, 77
of death, 26, 56
of existentialism, 34, 119,
120
of loneliness, 30, 56
of nihilism, 33, 101–102
of philosophical nature,
100–103, 105, 107,
109, 111–12, 115,
116, 120, 129
of psychological nature,
37, 54, 62–63, 66–67,
71–72, 73–74, 75, 77,
78
of sexual nature, 40–41
of terror, 2, 31, 92–93, 101
See also Affirmation of
life; Autobiographi-
cal elements; New
England, influence
of, on poetry; Prag-
matism
Theocritus, 52, 53
"There Are Roughly Zones,"
107
Thomas, Edward, 7, 12–13
Thompson, Lawrance, 2, 9,
30, 40

"Too Anxious for Rivers,"
107
"Trial by Existence, The,"
108–109, 111
Trilling, Lionel, 2, 33, 101
Turgenev, Ivan, influence
of, 54–55, 60
Twilight, 4
"Two Look at Two," 54

United Nations, 111–12
University of Michigan, 8
Untermeyer, Louis, corre-
spondence with, 9,
20, 25–26
U. S. State Department
goodwill missions, 10

Virgil, 52

Waiting for Godot (Beckett),
36
"West-Running Brook," 76,
109, 116–20
Whitman, Walt, 10, 102, 123
Will to Believe, The (Wil-
liam James), 103, 104
Winters, Yvor, and criticism
of Frost, 5, 100
"Witch of Coös, The," 13
"Wood-Pile, The," 7
Wordsworth, William, 32,
80, 106, 122–23, 127

Yeats, William Butler, 5, 23,
100, 128